the
JOURNEY
begins

RICK JOYNER

Updated & Expanded

$\mathcal{B}$ook

2

$\mathcal{T}$he $\mathcal{D}$ivine $\mathcal{D}$estiny Series

MorningStar
PUBLICATIONS

16000 Lancaster Highway
Charlotte, NC 28277-2061

The Journey Begins

by Rick Joyner

Copyright © 1992, 1997 by Rick Joyner.

All rights reserved.

Printed in the United States of America.

International Standard Book Number 1-878327-61-5.

Unless otherwise stated, all Scripture quotations are taken from the New American Standard Bible, copyright © 1960, 1962, 1963, 1968, 1971, 1973, 1974, 1977, by The Lockman Foundation. Italics in Scripture references are for emphasis only.

This book is dedicated to the MorningStar Ministry Team and MorningStar Fellowship in Charlotte. Together you have given me great confidence that there will be a church that completes the journey and becomes all that God has called her to be.

OTHER BOOKS BY RICK JOYNER:

Available in Hardcover:

The Divine Destiny Series:
There Were Two Trees in the Garden
The Journey Begins

The Final Quest
The Prophetic Ministry

Available in Softcover:

The Final Quest
The Surpassing Greatness of His Power
Epic Battles of the Last Days
There Were Two Trees in the Garden
The Journey Begins
The Harvest
The Harvest—Volume II
Leadership, Management and the Five Essentials for Success
The World Aflame
Visions of the Harvest

Combating Spiritual Strongholds Series:
    Overcoming the Accuser
    Overcoming the Spirit of Poverty
    Overcoming Racism
    Overcoming the Religious Spirit
    Overcoming Witchcraft

The Hall of Faith Series:
    The Three Witnesses
    Courage that Changed the World

Call 1-800-542-0278 to order or for a free catalog.

Table of Contents

Part III: God Gives His Written Word • 189

PREFACE

It is by grasping the whole plan of God that we can more fully understand any single part. An understanding of the overall plan of God will equip us to better understand the time in which we live and our own part in it. The greater our understanding of "the big picture," the more confidence we will have to fulfill our own mandate.

The Journey Begins is the second book in a planned seven-volume series, *The Divine Destiny*. When completed, this series will provide a comprehensive biblical overview of God's plan for this present age, as well as a biblical perspective of the age to come.

This series is not written just for serious Bible students, but for serious Christians—those committed to making their lives count by doing the will of God. The primary purpose of this series is to impart faith and confidence for the courageous and bold advance the church is destined to make at the end of this age.

Every Christian is meant to be a light in this world, to give illumination that reveals the glory of our God. The better we know His ways, the more boldly we will proclaim them. My prayer for this work is that it will stir every reader to sink their roots deeper into the Scriptures, seeking to know the Lord's ways because they love the Truth.

The first book in this series is entitled *There Were Two Trees in the Garden.* Though each book in this series has its own message and can be read and understood independently of the others, it is recommended that they be read in the proper order for the maximum benefit.

There Were Two Trees in the Garden ends with the deliverance of the people of God from bondage in Egypt and the beginning of their corporate walk with God after the Passover. This second volume starts as *The Journey Begins* and continues through the wilderness experiences meant to prepare Israel for the presence of God. In this volume we will seek a deeper understanding of our God and of all that must be accomplished in His people to prepare us for the conquest of our Promised Land.

Part I:
A Foundation
for Spiritual
Maturity

Chapter 1

THE RED
SEA BAPTISM

After more than four hundred years of slavery, Israel departed Egypt as a free people. Without a single weapon this humble band of slaves defeated the greatest nation on earth and carried away its treasure.

Even recognizing the dramatic changes taking place at the end of the twentieth century, there has never been a political reversal in human history to equal Israel's liberation from Egypt. Just days earlier, these slaves were without hope; then suddenly they were not only free but wealthier than even the most optimistic could have imagined. A truly marvelous God had considered their grief and had come to set them free.

Naturally, there was great rejoicing. The seed chosen to bring forth the Messiah had faced the seed of Cain in the most dramatic confrontation yet, and the victory had been overwhelming. But the victory was not yet complete. Pharaoh still had his army and he would use it to make one last bold attack upon the children of Israel.

In Pharaoh, we have one of the great biblical archetypes of Satan. Satan's highest priority continues to be keeping God's people in bondage. If he cannot keep us in bondage, he will try to destroy us. Our victory over him will not be complete until, like the Israelites who fled from Pharaoh, we have passed through the Red Sea. The Red Sea is a type, or biblical model, of baptism. It is through baptism that our enemy is to be utterly destroyed. Through baptism we are to be forever separated from the domain that has kept us in bondage. As the apostle Paul explained:

> **For I do not want you to be unaware, brethren, that our fathers were all under the cloud, and all passed through the sea;**

> **and all were baptized *INTO* Moses in the cloud and in the sea (I Corinthians 10:1- 2).**

> **Or do you not know that all of us who have been baptized *INTO* Christ Jesus have been baptized into His death? (Romans 6:3).**

As Pharaoh was a biblical type of Satan who seeks to keep us in bondage, Moses was the type of Christ who came to set us free. As stated in Corinthians, the Israelites were symbolically baptized into Moses by their experience at the

Red Sea, as a prophecy of how we are to be baptized into Christ Jesus.

True Baptism

What does it mean to be baptized into Christ? The word "baptize" literally means to be immersed. Paul said that Israel had been baptized *into* Moses in the cloud and in the sea and that in the same way we are baptized *into* Christ. To move *into* something is to be transferred from a position outside to a position inside. This is not a change of substance but a change of position. It is through baptism that we move from a position outside of Christ to a position of abiding in Him.

The Bible records how Israel was delivered from Egypt by the Passover, but it was through the Red Sea and being under the cloud in the wilderness that they were truly joined to Moses. Likewise, it is the cross that delivers us from bondage to the world, but it is through baptism and through following the cloud of God's presence that we are truly joined to Christ. Through baptism we move to a position *in* Him. Paul further elaborates on this in Romans 6:4-5:

> **Therefore we have been buried with Him through baptism into death, in order that as Christ was raised from the dead through the glory of the Father, so we too might walk in newness of life.**

> **For if we have become UNITED with Him in the likeness of His death, certainly we shall also be in the likeness of His resurrection.**

Note that in this key passage on baptism, there is *no mention of water*! Israel's passage through the Red Sea is a type of water baptism, which is a symbolic ritual that represents the true baptism. Baptism is being united with Christ in the very likeness of His death in order to live in the power of His resurrection. We can immerse a person in water as many times as we like—in the name of the Father, Son and Holy Spirit, or in the name of Jesus—but it will never, by itself, make us partakers of the Lord's death. Water baptism is a ritual that represents a commitment we are making to live in union with Christ.

Just as a wedding ceremony is not the actual marriage but rather a ceremonial commitment to marriage, water baptism is a ceremonial commitment to what is supposed to become a reality in our lives. The baptism that Paul was declaring to the Roman Christians was the actual commitment to union with the Lord in His death. This is a day by day commitment to take up our crosses and lay down our own lives and self-interests for the sake of the gospel.

This baptism was a total reality, not just the comprehension of a doctrine or a submission to a ritual. This is the true baptism, daily laying down our own lives and interests to serve Him. Our immersion in water is a ceremonial ritual that symbolizes our pledge to make our total commitment to Jesus a reality, testifying that we will no longer live for ourselves but for Him.

This is not to any way belittle the importance of water baptism. God-ordained ceremonies are important, just as a wedding ceremony is important for the proper beginning of a marriage. Water baptism is given far more importance in the New Testament than most contemporary churches have recognized. The first Christians did not practice the modern invention known as "the altar call." Immediately after conversion the new believers were baptized by immersion in water. They did this just as quickly as they could find water.

The practice of taking new converts immediately to the water is often inconvenient, but that is one of the important reasons for it. We must begin our walk with Christ with the commitment not to be ruled by convenience, but by His will. Our submission to convenience is possibly the greatest foe to our entering into the true baptism—laying down our lives for His sake.

How much more meaningful would the conversion experience be if we laid aside our modern substitutes for water baptism and returned to the scriptural mandate? How many more people would begin their spiritual walks on a firmer footing, understanding the essential commitment to lay down their lives and sacrifice their own convenience? If we connected conversion with an immediate demonstration of how important the church considers obedience to God's mandate in His Word, wouldn't our converts gain a much more solid foundation?

Even science has proven that the quality of our birth can powerfully affect our whole lives. When the birth procedure described as "drug them and tug them" was implemented— which meant drugging the mother and tugging out the baby—that generation grew up in the 1960s and 1970s and released a drug culture that has swept the world. In the same way, the quality of our conversion can have an impact on the quality of our entire spiritual lives.

Our worship of convenience is a terrible enemy of the true faith. It is one of the first idols that must be destroyed in our lives if we are going to abide in Christ. Therefore it is important that we return to the biblical practice of sealing the new birth with baptism—and quickly! In doing this we must also impart a clear understanding of what this baptism represents.

Making Ritual Reality

Again, as important as water baptism is, we must understand that fulfilling the ritual is not necessarily the same as *fulfilling* the covenant; it is merely the equivalent of *signing* the covenant. Better off is the one who, though never accomplishing the ritual, fulfills the covenant, than the one who religiously fulfills the ritual but fails to lay down his life.

The act of water baptism does not save us; it does not cleanse us; it causes no one to partake of the Lord's death, which is the true baptism. Yet, the reality of what water baptism symbolizes *does* accomplish all these things, as Peter explained:

For it is better, if God should will it so, that you suffer for doing what is right rather than for doing what is wrong.

For Christ also died for sins once for all, the just for the unjust, in order that He might bring us to God, having been put to death in the flesh, but made alive in the spirit;

in which also He went and made proclamation to the spirits in prison,

who once were disobedient, when the patience of God kept waiting in the days of Noah, during the construction of the ark, in which a few, that is, eight persons, were brought safely through the water.

And corresponding to that, BAPTISM NOW SAVES YOU—not the removal of dirt from the flesh, but the appeal to God for a good conscience—THROUGH THE RESURRECTION OF JESUS CHRIST (I Peter 3:17-21).

True baptism *does* save us—but the baptism ritual of being immersed in water is only symbolic of a greater reality. We are submerged in order to represent laying down our own lives to share in His death, and then rising out of the water to represent that we are also partaking of His resurrection.

For if we have become united with Him in the likeness of His death, certainly we shall be also in the likeness of His resurrection (Romans 6:5).

Chapter 2

Death Is the Path to Life

What did the Lord mean when He stated, **"I have come to cast a fire upon the earth; and how I wish it were already kindled! But I have a baptism to undergo, and how distressed I am until it is accomplished!"** (Luke 12:49-50)? Was the baptism that was distressing Him simply being immersed in water? Of course not. He was referring to His impending crucifixion. That crucifixion is also the meaning of our baptism.

Jesus was also referring to the baptism into His crucifixion when James and John asked to be seated on His right and left in the kingdom. He replied, **"You do not know what you are asking for. Are you able to drink the cup that**

I drink, or to be baptized with the baptism with which I am baptized?" (Mark 10:38)

To be baptized with His baptism is to be conformed to the purpose of His death and to lay down our own lives for the sake of others. Reducing this to a mere ritual robs the Lord of our true consecration and the church of its salvation. It has stolen from the world the power of the gospel. Many Scriptures verify and further articulate this meaning. Following are just a few of them:

> For if we *died with Him* we shall also live with Him; If we *endure,* we shall also reign with Him (II Timothy 2:11-12).

> The Spirit Himself bears witness with our spirit that we are the children of God,
>
> and if children, heirs also, heirs of God and fellow heirs with Christ, IF INDEED WE SUFFER WITH HIM *IN ORDER THAT* we may also be glorified with Him (Romans 8:16-17).

> That I may know Him, and the power of His resurrection and the FELLOWSHIP OF HIS SUFFER-INGS, being conformed to His death;

> *IN ORDER THAT* I may attain to the resurrection from the dead (Philippians 3:10-11).

> For to you it has been granted for Christ's sake, not only to believe in Him, but also to *suffer* for His sake (Philippians 1:29).

We ought always to give thanks to God for you, brethren, as is only fitting, because your faith is greatly enlarged, and the love of each one of you toward one another grows ever greater;

therefore, we ourselves speak proudly of you among the churches of God for your perseverance and faith in the midst of all your *persecutions* and *afflictions* which you endure.

This is a plain indication of God's righteous judgment so that you may be considered worthy of the kingdom of God, for which indeed you are *suffering* (II Thessalonians 1:3-5).

We are *afflicted* in every way, but not crushed; perplexed, but not despairing;

persecuted, but not forsaken; struck down but not destroyed;

ALWAYS carrying about in the body the dying of Jesus, that the life of Jesus also may be manifested in our body.

For we who live are constantly being delivered over to *death* for Jesus' sake, that the life of Jesus also may be manifested in our mortal flesh (II Corinthians 4:8-11).

The Lord made it clear in His Word that if we are to partake of His *life* we must also partake of His *death*. Any other teaching is a false gospel and an enemy of the cross. Death separates the things that are natural from the things that are spiritual. To have a resurrection there must first be a death.

If we want to walk in the resurrection life of Jesus we must be willing to lay down our lives for Him.

In the first century, some of the people thought that if they would circumcise their flesh they would be right with God; but He requires the circumcision of our *hearts*. There are those today who point to the day of their immersion as the day they died with Jesus and were resurrected. Every ritual of our faith is just that—a ritual, something meant to symbolize a commitment to the spiritual reality of which it speaks. In Christ we must die daily in order to live. The ritual was but the commitment to do this. As the Lord Jesus Himself testified:

> **If anyone wishes to come after Me, let him deny himself, and take up his cross, and follow Me.**

> **For whoever wishes to save his life shall lose it; but whoever loses his life for My sake shall find it (Matthew 16:24-25).**

We Were Tricked!

Interestingly, the Israelites did not go to their baptism willingly. The Lord had to trick them into it, as we read in Exodus 13:17-18 and 14:1-4:

> **Now it came about when Pharaoh let the people go that God did not lead them by way of the land of the Philistines, even though it was near; for God said, "Lest the people change their minds when they see war, and they return to Egypt."**

> **Hence God led the people around by the way of the wilderness to the Red Sea...**
>
> **Now the LORD spoke to Moses, saying, "Tell the sons of Israel to turn back and camp before Pi-hahiroth, between Migdol and the sea...**
>
> **"For Pharaoh will say of the sons of Israel, 'They are wandering aimlessly in the land; the wilderness has shut them in.'**
>
> **"Thus I will harden Pharaoh's heart, and he will chase after them; and I will be honored through Pharaoh and all his army, and the Egyptians will know that I am the LORD." And they did so.**

Can you relate to this? The only way the Lord could get Israel to partake of baptism was to trick them into it. Are not most of our experiences just like this? The Lord so aligns our circumstances that there is absolutely no way out but to lay down our lives and conform to the image of His death. Unless we lay down our lives for Him, we will face the enemy's lancers. It may be at our job, in our family, or even in the church, but there is a divine trap laid for us all, and the only way of escape is to lay down our lives.

The Israelites panicked when they saw the army of Egypt coming after them. They quickly challenged both Moses' and God's intentions. Many of us are amazed at the unbelief of the Israelites during the time of their deliverance from Egypt and their wilderness journey. But we need to consider their circumstances before we judge them too harshly. All of their experiences are a parallel or prophetic foreshadowing of the experiences we all go through in our Christian walks. Looking back, most of us who have walked with the Lord a while must now confess to many of the same failures that they experienced.

It is true that Israel had witnessed great miracles in Egypt. Even so, signs were commonly performed by sorcerers in those days. Some of the Lord's miracles were duplicated by Pharaoh's witch doctors. The Israelites did not have the Bible, and for four hundred years all they knew of the Lord was from legends or stories passed down from their ancestors. After four hundred years without hearing from God, who would not begin to doubt?

Even when He did reveal Himself, they knew little about His character. All they knew was that He was more powerful than the demons of Egypt. They probably wanted to believe the best about Him, yet it must have been a fearful experience to have this powerful God come and snatch them out of Egypt. Then imagine what it would be like to stand defenseless with your wives and children as the most powerful army in the world bears down on you and your back is to the sea! It is not hard to understand why they would challenge Moses and begin to wonder if this God they knew so little about had just led them out to make sport of them.

It has been easy for us to scorn Israel's behavior at the Red Sea, but we have little room to talk. For if those at the Red Sea and the wilderness journey could look down through the centuries at the modern-day church, they would see that we have been willing to do almost anything to escape pain or inconvenience. They would no doubt marvel that we are such softies! It was not easy for them, and it is not easy for us. They had to be led to a place where there simply was no alternative but to be "baptized" in the Red Sea.

The Lord usually has to do the same to us. It was a trying experience for them and it will usually be one for us too, *but it is the path to the Promised Land!* This is our salvation—baptism into the Lord's death is the gateway to resurrection life. God has traps set for us, but they are all for the purpose that we might know His salvation. As we experience the continual parting of the Red Seas in our lives, our faith in the power of His salvation constantly grows.

The Destruction of Our Enemy

There is another great benefit to our baptism. The trap that is set by God for us is also an ambush for our enemies. It was at the Red Sea that the tormentors and oppressors of Israel, the legions of Egypt, would be utterly destroyed.

> The LORD said to Moses, "Stretch out your hand over the sea so that the waters may come back over the Egyptians, over their chariots and their horsemen."
>
> So Moses stretched out his hand over the sea, and the sea returned to its normal state at daybreak, while the Egyptians were fleeing right into it; then the LORD overthrew the Egyptians in the midst of the sea.

And the waters returned and covered the chariots and the horsemen, even the Pharaoh's entire army that had gone into the sea after them; NOT EVEN ONE OF THEM REMAINED (Exodus 14:26-28).

When the Lord laid down His life at the cross, it was the doom of the enemy. As we are baptized into the Lord's death we enter into the one place that Satan and his hosts cannot follow. The very cross that results in resurrection life and power for the saints results in the lake of fire for Satan and his cohorts. When the body of Christ enters into its baptism on the scale that the Lord has prepared for the end of the age, there is going to be a manifestation of the power of the cross that will utterly consume Satan's hosts.

What appeared to be their doom was actually Israel's salvation. That which appears to be our end will *always* result in our salvation too: **"But thanks be to God, who always leads us in His triumph in Christ" (II Corinthians 2:14).** We must learn to rejoice when we are closed in and there seems to be no escape. At the proper time the door will open which leads to the Promised Land.

Death to self-will, to self-promotion, to self-seeking is the path to the greatest freedom and release of spirit we will ever know. If we are dead to this world what can the world do to us? It is impossible for a dead man to feel rejection, insecurity, insult or fear. When we have entered into the true baptism we are freed from the bondage of anything the world can inflict upon us. Satan can no longer have any dominion over us.

As the proverb states, "A coward dies a thousand deaths, but a man of courage dies only once." When we enter into the true baptism so **"that they who live should no longer live for themselves, but for Him" (II Corinthians 5:15),** we die to the self-will in our lives. We may die daily, but there is no more pain in it, because we are already dead. Then our fears, which are rooted in self-preservation, are removed. We are given a courage and peace which goes beyond human comprehension. We are **"always carrying about in the body the dying of Jesus, that the life of Jesus also may be manifested in our body" (II Corinthians 4:10).**

When we comprehend what we gain by laying down our lives, we will understand James' exhortation to **"Consider it all joy, my brethren, when you encounter various trials, knowing that the testing of your faith produces endurance. And let endurance have its perfect result, that you may be perfect and complete, lacking in nothing" (James 1:2-4).** Every time we lay down our lives for the sake of the gospel and the cross, we enter a little more into the power of resurrection life. Death cannot touch resurrection life; it is this life that utterly destroys the enemy's power over us. We must embrace the cross!

Chapter 3

RESURRECTION LIFE

Baptism is the laying down of our own lives to die to our own wills and self-interests. We die in Christ in order to live. If this death is actually the end of us, we are the greatest of fools—all our preaching is in vain (I Corinthians 15:14). But this death is not the end—*it is the beginning!* We have eternal life! Life is our ministry and gospel.

The Lord overcame death by dying, and we do the same. Though baptism is a death, we enter it so that we can overcome the power it has over us. Accompanying our death to self will be an awesome release of resurrection life.

Believing in the Resurrection

Charles Spurgeon was called "the prince of preachers" and is considered one of the best preachers of all time. He once made the remarkable observation that, *"There are very few Christians who believe in the resurrection."* When I first read that statement I thought it was a misprint, or at least something that had been taken out of context. How could someone be a Christian and not believe in the resurrection? However, after some pondering, I knew there was truth in Spurgeon's statement.

There is a difference between giving intellectual and doctrinal assent to the fact of the resurrection and having faith in the resurrection. There is a big difference between believing in our minds and believing in our hearts. *If we really believed in our hearts the truth of the resurrection, our lives would be radically different from the lives of most Christians today.*

Many Christians are under the delusion that mere intellectual agreement with certain biblical or historical facts constitutes true faith. This has caused many to feel safe in a spiritual condition in which their eternal lives may still be in jeopardy. The apostle Paul clarified this issue when he wrote to the Romans:

> **If you confess with your mouth Jesus as Lord** *and* **believe in your heart that God raised Him from the dead, you shall be saved;**
>
> **for with** *the heart* **man believes, resulting in righteousness (Romans 10:9-10).**

One widely accepted reference book, *Funk & Wagnal's Standard Handbook of Synonyms, Antonyms and Prepositions,* defines faith as "a union of belief and trust; *it is a belief so strong that it becomes a part of one's own nature."* Although a secular reference book has no authority to establish doctrine, this definition of faith is consistent with biblical truth. True faith is more than just an intellectual assumption or preference— true faith impacts and directs our lives or it is not real.

The Nature of True Faith

Faith is stronger than mere belief. To believe is simply to give intellectual assent to something; to have faith is to be inseparable from the object of our devotion. While belief can be changed when confronted with a persuasive argument, true faith is so much a part of the person that it can be taken only by death.

Our faith is who we are. It is the substance of our very existence and identity. The stronger the faith of the believer, the stronger his existence, and the more impact he will have on the world he touches.

This difference between "faith" and "belief" is the difference between being a true Christian and being a pretender who has deluded himself in order to appease his conscience. The popular and pervasive view of "believing in God"—meaning that we simply believe that He exists—is not the faith of the Scriptures. This can be the *beginning* of faith, but it is far less than the true Christian faith. The notion that we just need to believe *He exists* in order to be saved is a tragic delusion. It is a lie that keeps many from genuine faith in God.

A person without true faith is like a car without an engine; it may have a beautiful appearance but it will not get you anywhere. The stronger the faith, the further and the faster we will go. Belief alone is superficial, and by itself accomplishes little more than possibly appeasing our conscience. Faith is a living power which can move the mountains that stand in its way.

Moses led Israel into the wilderness in order to convert her superstitions and shallow beliefs into a rock solid faith. Our wilderness, the trials that we endure to test our faith, is meant to accomplish the same in us. If we respond properly to our wilderness, it will turn whatever degree of faith that we have into a powerful force. We must embrace our difficulties as opportunities if we are to get to the Promised Land. We must not let the difficulties discourage us, or we too will perish in our wilderness and never realize our goal and purpose in the Lord.

Trials Are the Door to Freedom

Moses could lead Israel out of Egypt, but he could not take Egypt out of the Israelites. The difficulties of the wilderness were designed to do that. The Israelites had been slaves in Egypt. Though slavery is the most base human condition, there is a perverted kind of security in slavery that is hard to relinquish. Even though the conditions may be harsh, a slave does not have to deal with the many difficult decisions that freedom requires. Even though the Israelites were freed and actually moving toward the fulfillment of their destiny, most of them began looking back to Egypt with longing in their hearts when they encountered difficulties. They actually desired the oppression and harshness of slavery over having to walk in freedom, which requires true faith.

This is why many who were recently freed from the terrible oppression of communism are calling for a return to the old order. This is the dividing line that separates those who go on to victory from those who go back to their doom. No one will attain his spiritual destiny until he becomes *free*. The free man would rather perish in the wilderness trying to fulfill his destiny than go back to slavery.

Until we make the decision that we will not go back, regardless of how painful it gets, we will not go forward with the force of faith that it will take to fulfill our destiny. Jesus once declared, **"No one, after putting his hand to the plow and looking back, is fit for the kingdom of God"** (Luke 9:62). If we are still looking back, we are not ready to go forward.

The Language of Bondage

The most telltale symptom of surrender to slavery is grumbling and complaining. The one who complains has lost the faith—he has already given up in his heart. The one with true faith views even the most severe obstacles as opportunities to win greater victories and make a greater advance toward his goal.

True faith is not blind optimism. That kind of optimism is but one more intellectual assessment masquerading as the true faith. Humanistic optimism will wither in the heat of the desert wilderness, while true faith will become stronger and more determined as the heat of the fiery trials increases.

Faith is able to move mountains, and it will move every one that stands in its way. True faith makes a road where there is none. That is why true faith is true freedom; *no* shackle can be put on it. It is the ability to seize the vision of our destiny with such a grip that it cannot be taken away until it is fulfilled. Such faith moves every obstacle, but is moved by no obstacle. True faith *will* get to the Promised Land.

Let us understand one important fact about true faith: True faith is *not* faith in *our* faith! True faith has an Object and a Source of power that is greater than itself. True faith is not measured by the quality of "our faith." Such a measurement is just another form of self-centeredness and self-seeking. Instead, it is measured by our trust in God. The use of any other measuring device is worse than a pretension—it is a deception.

Inevitably, those whose faith is in themselves only accomplish what is selfish. Self-centeredness has proven to be a sure door to deception. In the beginning, when Adam and Eve ate of the forbidden fruit, the first fruit of their sin was that they immediately began to focus upon themselves; they looked at their own condition and focused on their own nakedness. Self-centeredness is always the result when we eat from the deadly Tree of Knowledge, and it is slavery in its most base form. The self-centered are an emotionally crippled people. When we start looking to ourselves we will fall from grace and lose the power of true faith.

Stephen W. Hawking is reputedly one of the greatest thinkers of our time. He is considered by many to be an even greater theorist than Einstein. He is said to have the potential to grasp answers to questions that other great scientists have not yet even been able to ask. This brilliant man stated that his quest is simply "trying to understand the mind of God."

Finding the mind of God is the reason for our lives and the object and source of all true faith. Anything less than seeking the purpose ordained by God is not worthy of the intelligent expenditure of energy or time. Only when we find God's plan and possess it with true faith will we be fulfilled.

The apostle Paul would also have to be included as one of the most brilliant men of all time. It is Paul who exhorts us to **"study to show thyself approved unto God [not men]"** (II Timothy 2:15 KJV). True study cannot be self-centered or man-centered; it must be God-centered.

When we have direction from God, the Source of reality itself, a power is released called *faith*, and nothing in the rest of creation can stand in its way. There is no greater motivation than that of knowing our calling, a destiny that is rooted in the plan of God from the beginning. There is no greater power available than that which is found in having this resolve. This is faith.

The True Temple

The faith of the apostles was devoted to building a temple for God that could not be made with human hands. This temple could only be contained in human hearts. The church they built was composed of people who had true faith. This church was not an organization, but a living organism; it was not an institution, but a constitution. The apostolic vision was God living in people—not bricks.

Just as shallow scientific men used the profound discoveries of Einstein to build nuclear bombs-- the most terrible vehicles of destruction—shallow religious men have used the profound gospel teachings related to the true faith to create empty rituals and forms that destroy men's souls. When a believer grasps the true faith, he does not *go to* church; he *becomes* the church. The true church is a source of power and life that no building or institution can contain. Only a human heart that has been purified by faith is great enough to contain this power and life.

Reality is not found in ritual. True faith is a river of life too powerful to be contained in the structures in which men have often tried to contain it. There are gatherings, or congregations, of those who share a real and powerful faith. *Some* of these gatherings take place in institutional churches. Those who possess the real faith are inevitably drawn to the most real people who live on this earth.

We all receive strengthening when we are joined to others with true faith. But true faith does not worship the temple of

God; it worships the God of the temple. When those who are true believers are asked about their faith, they do not point to a building, an organization, a set of doctrines, or even to concepts about truth—they point to the true God.

As the apostle Paul explained, **"The kingdom of God does not consist in words, but in power" (I Corinthians 4:20).** The apostles and prophets foresaw a house of true faith, not being built *by* people but being built *out of people*. Those whose lives are being built on the true faith will easily recognize other people who are also part of the same faith. They are recognizable, not by their creeds or alliances, but by the power and character of the One who has imparted true faith to them. Church is not something you go to; church is something you become. We must not settle for anything less.

It is reported that when Napoleon read the Gospel of John he declared that either Jesus was the Son of God, or else the one who wrote this Gospel was! Napoleon recognized that the genius of true Christianity was far beyond the creative powers of any human genius. He then looked at the institution of Christianity and saw no relationship between the gospel and what he saw in the institution. There often is no relationship between the substance of truth and what men who do not have the true faith try to do with it. Just as the most religious and upstanding citizens were the ones who crucified Jesus, the most religious and upstanding institutions are often the ones that continue trying to destroy true faith in Jesus.

But true faith will not die in an institution. True faith is an indestructible power that will live forever. That power was able to transform just a few fishermen and humble folk into the greatest force in history. This force challenged Rome, the most powerful empire in history, and unraveled it. True faith is a power that took a few letters written by these simple men and impacted history more than all other books combined. Just a small portion of true faith in your life will radically transform you and your destiny. From the most noble and far-reaching human ideals, to the biggest nuclear weapon, no force in history has demonstrated the power of true faith to change the world.

But we must beware! Only the most courageous have pressed beyond the muddied waters of the pretender faith to taste the pure waters of the true. God intended for it to be that way. The power of true faith is too great to entrust to anyone but those who will esteem it as their most precious possession. Such is the constitution of all who would rise above mediocrity to the highest place and taste the fruit of the Promised Land of God. The wilderness is meant to bring out either the best or the worst in man. Each of us decides which it will be.

Paul's exhortation was to **"Test yourselves to see if you are in the faith; examine yourselves!" (II Corinthians 13:5)** The overemphasis upon *what* we believe instead of *how* we believe has resulted in many becoming more like parrots than like Christ. It does little good to say the right things if our lives are not changed.

Chapter 4

THE APOSTOLIC COMMISSION

In Acts 1:22 we see that the apostolic office was for the purpose of being **"a witness...of His resurrection."** The message of the resurrection was to be the basis of the apostolic gospel. Yet it seems clear that the general gospel message that is preached today is producing little true faith in the resurrection. Why?

I searched through my library for messages on the resurrection by those who are considered some of the greatest men of faith since biblical times. I was shocked by what I found. In the numerous volumes of teaching and insight produced by these distinguished leaders, I rarely found more than a page or two on the subject of the resurrection! And many of these references to the resurrection were obviously just obligatory Easter sermons.

With several centuries of emphasis upon recovering biblical truth, how is it that this foundational truth upon which the gospel is based could be so neglected? Is it not time to again recover the meaning and power of the resurrection?

As I studied the enigma of great men of God seemingly avoiding the issue of the resurrection, it became apparent why this message has been so neglected. The faith and power of the first-century church was the result of their faith in the resurrection, *but it was this faith and their testimony of the resurrection that resulted in the persecution they experienced.*

When Peter and John were dragged before the Sanhedrin, they were arrested because the rulers were **"being greatly disturbed because they (Peter and John) were teaching the people and proclaiming in Jesus *the resurrection from the dead"* (Acts 4:2).** When Paul was later arrested and brought before this same board, he declared, *"I am on trial for the hope and resurrection of the dead!"* (Acts 23:6)

Probably nothing will bring persecution upon us faster than preaching the message of the resurrection. When we begin to preach this message we are attacking Satan's strongest fortress, his most powerful grip upon this world and the church—*the fear of death.* There is no truth which will set us more free than the truth of the resurrection. A man released from the fear of death will be free indeed. This freedom is a prerequisite to complete freedom in any other area of our lives. The witness of the resurrection was, and still is, the basic message of the apostolic gospel.

There is more Scripture devoted to Abraham's finding a burial place than is devoted to such important subjects as being born again. Every word in Scripture is important—not a single "jot or tittle" is wasted. Why, then, is this so important? Why did Isaac and Jacob insist on being buried in the same place? Why would Joseph make Israel swear to carry up his bones to bury him there? And why was this request listed in Hebrews 11 as one of the great acts of faith?

What difference did it make where these men of faith were buried? The place of this burial sight was Hebron, a town just south of Jerusalem. We can see the answer when we read Matthew's account of the crucifixion of Jesus:

> **And Jesus cried out again with a loud voice, and yielded up His spirit.**
>
> **And behold, the veil of the temple was torn in two from top to bottom, and the earth shook; and the rocks were split,**
>
> **and the tombs were opened;** *and many of the bodies of the saints who had fallen asleep were raised* **(Matthew 27:50-52).**

These heroes of faith had prophetically foreseen the crucifixion and resurrection of Jesus, and had positioned themselves to be a part of it! The Lord Himself confirmed this when He said, **"Your father Abraham desired to see My day, and he** *saw* **it and was glad" (John 8:56).**

When the **"eyes of our hearts"** (**Ephesians 1:18**) are opened, we begin to see the things that are eternal. We are no longer bound by time and by the things which are temporal. Abraham saw with the eyes of his heart. Therefore, he could look ahead to see the crucifixion and resurrection of Jesus. Abraham, looking ahead, was able to believe in Him who was to come just as we believe in Him looking back in history.

When we begin to see with the eyes of our hearts instead of just our natural eyes, we not only begin to see the things that are eternal, but they become *more real* to us than the things which are temporary. Then, like Abraham, we will not become overly possessive of anything in the temporary realm. We will freely give back to God even the chosen purposes of God in our lives-- our "Isaacs"—because we know that the resurrection will give them back to us for eternity.

Abraham had seen the day of the Lord and he understood that Isaac was a "type" (Hebrews 11:19) or prophetic model of the coming Messiah. That is why he made Isaac carry the wood for his own sacrifice, just as Jesus was to bear His own cross. That is why he could so confidently say **"God will provide for Himself the lamb" (Genesis 22:8).** When we have the eyes of our hearts opened to see the purpose and plan of God, a faith is imparted to live a radically different life, a life free from the bonds of temporal concerns.

Opening the Eyes of Our Hearts

But how do we get this faith so that the eyes of our hearts are opened? How do we get our intellectual understanding of biblical truths transferred from our minds to our hearts? The answer to this question is utterly practical. We must develop a *secret* relationship with God.

Jesus asked His followers, **"How can you believe, when you receive glory from one another, and you do not seek the glory that is from the one and only God?" (John 5:44)** Jesus knew that one of the most destructive factors undermining true faith is our desire for human recognition, so He emphatically warned us against it:

> **Beware of practicing your righteousness before men to be noticed by them;** *otherwise you have no reward with your Father who is in heaven.*
>
> **When therefore you give alms, do not sound a trumpet before you, as the hypocrites do in the synagogues and in the streets, that they may be honored by men. Truly I say to you, they have their reward in full.**
>
> **But when you give alms, do not let your left hand know what your right hand is doing that your alms may be in secret; and your Father** *who sees in secret* **will repay you.**
>
> **And when you pray, you are not to be as the hypocrites; for they love to stand and pray in the synagogues and on the street corners, in order to be seen by men. Truly I say to you, they have their reward in full.**

But you, when you pray, go into your inner room, and when you have shut your door, *pray to your Father who is in secret, and your Father who sees in secret will repay you* **(Matthew 6:1-6).**

Typically, some of the most devoted servants, the most faithful intercessors and the most generous contributors to the Lord's purposes have little or no reward saved up in heaven. This is because they seek human recognition for their deeds on earth. When we do this, we receive our reward "in full." If we really believe in the resurrection, and really understand that we are laying up fruit for eternal life, we will not waste an eternal inheritance on trivial and fleeting human recognition and honor.

On the contrary, the one who really believes in the resurrection in his heart becomes increasingly focused on laying up fruit for eternal life. When we really believe, we will begin to build that secret relationship with the Father, not wanting anyone but our Father to know about our alms or prayers. When our treasure really is being deposited in our "heavenly bank account," then where our treasure is there will our heart be also. *When our hearts are with the Father in heaven, the eyes of our hearts start to open, and those things which are eternal become more real to us than the things which are passing away.* This deep, life changing process explains an important factor in the nature of true faith.

"Seed faith" teachings are biblical and true. However, when we set our eyes on reaping "things above" instead of things on earth, we do not give in order to get a bigger house, a better car, or a more important job. We give in order to receive even more seed, so we can do more sowing. Those who have set their affections on things above do not want to cash the checks from their spiritual bank account on the things which are temporal. They would rather give to the work of bringing more souls into the kingdom of God, so they can reap their fruit in heaven.

Once we have truly seen with our hearts what Jesus has done for us, we will want to do everything for Him. Our passion will be to see Him receive the reward of His sacrifice. When we see what He has done for us, how can we be selfishly ambitious with our heavenly treasures?

By the Lord's grace, He delivered us from slavery to the world, but He purchased us to be His slaves. We are to no longer live for ourselves, but for Him (II Corinthians 5:15). Even though we are His slaves, He pays us better than any human agency ever could. As we help lead others into His kingdom, and then support them and seek their spiritual prosperity, we partake of their fruit *forever*!

When we begin to *really* believe in the resurrection and the eternal inheritance we have in Christ, there is no place for jealousy or territorial preservation. If someone comes to our town with a greater anointing, we are foolish not to pray for them! We should do everything possible to support and help their ministry, because through our prayers we can partake of the fruit of their ministry for eternity. When we begin to see eternity and live for the eternal, we will then pray for other ministries and hope that they succeed and even surpass us in fruitfulness.

When we really believe in the resurrection, we do not care who gets the attention or recognition on earth. Our treasures are in heaven. Heaven is where our heart is, and heaven is where we want our reward. This life is but a vapor when compared to eternity. Who cares what we get here! When we really begin to believe this with a true faith that sees the eternal more clearly than the temporal, we will begin to watch over and protect one another's ministries, instead of trying to belittle or tear them down out of jealousy or intimidation.

It is not wrong for us to labor for the reward. The Scripture states that even Jesus endured the cross **"for the joy set before Him" (Hebrews 12:2).** To do things for the sake of the reward is neither wrong nor evil. However, there are more noble motives for our labor. We come to know these as our love for the Lord grows.

The joy for which Jesus endured the cross was basically twofold. First, He desired to obey and please His Father, not for His own sake, but because the Father deserved it. Secondly, Jesus loves us just as the Father loves us, and it is His joy to see our joy as we are reconciled to the Father and partake of His inheritance with Him.

It is right to rejoice in our own reward, just as it is right for children to rejoice in gifts from their parents. However, the chief joy will come when we hear the Lord say to us, **"Well** done, good and faithful slave" (Matthew 25:21). Then we will see face to face the joy *He receives* from the redemption of those for whom we labored in His name.

For all eternity, it will be the joy of the Lord, not just our joy, that will be our purpose and our passion. We can bring Him joy today by believing in Him and in His resurrection, devoting ourselves to that secret relationship He wants to have with each one of us. The joy of the Lord is our strength.

What Is Life?

One of the oldest theological and philosophical questions is, "What is life?" Basically, *life is communication.* All living things, whether plant or animal, are alive only as long as they communicate, or interrelate with their environment. As long as something breathes the air, partakes of food, and returns waste, it is alive. When this interrelationship stops, it is dead.

Entities are considered a higher life form if they have the capacity to communicate on higher levels. For example, a dog is considered a higher life form than a plant because it can understand commands, recognize people, etc. Humans are considered higher life forms than animals because we can communicate on higher levels.

Spiritual life is a higher life form than physical life. We are alive spiritually as long as we communicate or interrelate in the spirit. Jesus is the Word of God, or the very Communication of God. If we are in communication with Him in the Spirit, our bodies can be killed but our lives cannot be destroyed. Then our lives exist on a spiritual level that cannot be touched in this present realm. As the Lord said, **"I am the resurrection and the life; he who believes in [literally "into"] Me shall live even if he dies, and everyone who lives and believes in Me shall never die" (John 11:25-26).**

Jesus came that we might have this life and have it more abundantly (John 10:10). **"This is eternal life, that they may KNOW Thee [the Father], the only true God, and Jesus Christ whom Thou has sent" (John 17:3).** Jesus did not say that eternal life was found in knowing *about* Him, but in actually knowing Him. We can know a lot about someone without actually knowing them personally. It is possible to meet Him personally, and even have many contacts with Him, yet not abide in Him or maintain our spiritual communication and interrelationship with Him.

Many come to know Jesus as the Way. A few more go on to know Him as the Truth. But very few go on to know Him as their Life. If we seek the way, that may be all we find. If we seek the truth, that may be all we find. If we seek to know Jesus as our Life, we will know the way and the truth as well.

Life is the issue. It is the Tree of Life that we must partake of. It is the Path of Life that we must walk. It is only when we have come to understand true Life that we can really understand how death is the path to life in Christ. Without knowing this Life, the death of baptism will be meaningless. Paul explained to the Corinthians that without love, even giving our bodies to be burned will not profit us.

I knew two teenage girls who went to visit an elderly lady. They were distraught when they saw the dreariness of her small apartment and learned of the loneliness of her existence. When they told her how sorry they were for her in that situation, she looked at them in amazement. "Young ladies," she said, "do you see these bare walls? They are walls of praise because Jesus abides in this place!"

Suddenly the girls saw in that woman a light and a life that made them feel petty and empty by comparison. The elderly woman was actually feeling sorry for them! This woman had never known loneliness because she dwelt in the presence of the Lord. What many would view as an intolerable existence, she was able to see as a joy and an opportunity to draw closer to the Lord. For those who enter into true baptism it is the same. Their attention will not be on death, but the opportunity to enter a greater life. Those young girls ended up having the woman pray for *them*!

When we begin to live according to the life of the Son of God, all baptisms become doors that are embraced with expectation and joy (James 1:2-4). The more we die, the more we live. This is what comes from conquering death. This is the Lake of Fire that consumes all our enemies. In baptism, we do not die just to die; we gladly lay down our old life so that death will be swallowed up in LIFE. With each death we grasp more firmly that which is eternal life—union with our Father and His Son.

The more we enter this devotion to eternal life, the more we will embrace as opportunities the trials that cause us to press into Him. He is so much more to be desired than anything the world can offer.

The First Test of the Kingdom

Solomon and his reign are a prophetic type of the coming kingdom of God on earth. After he became king, Solomon's very first test was over the question of *life* (I Kings 3:16-28). Solomon had the wisdom to know how to identify the real mother of the living infant by determining which woman had the highest regard for the infant's life. The one having the least regard for this infant's life would be the one prone to carelessness with her own child, that could have led to accidently smothering him.

Likewise, as we seek to enter and abide in the kingdom, this will be our first test to determine whether we are authentic or pretenders. A sword will be drawn on the life that is given to us. We too must be willing to give it up before we can receive it back. It is shocking how many would willingly see that life die rather than give up their control of it.

Those of this nature, trying to hold on to what they have, are always left with nothing. If we seek to save our life we lose it. If we will lose our life for His sake, we will truly find it (Matthew 16:25). The real mother gave up her child so that he could live, but by doing this she received him back from the king. Sometimes the best way to protect and receive what

God has for us is to give it up. We must have the highest regard for life, but this regard cannot be possessive.

The Lord will remove carelessness from our nature so that we can properly handle this treasure. As we understand that life is communication we begin to see how **"death and life are in the power of the tongue" (Proverbs 18:21)**, and **"the mouth of the righteous is a fountain of life" (Proverbs 10:11)**. It is for this reason that **"every careless word that men shall speak, they shall render account for it in the day of judgment" (Matthew 12:36)**.

Our words give life or death; let us handle them with the utmost care. Are we imparting faith or fear, patience or discord, obedience or rebellion? Are we speaking by the Spirit of God or the spirit of the world? How are we handling the life that is given to us? The words we speak reveal the spirit that we are abiding in. If we are partaking of the Tree of Life, then our words will impart life, for a good tree will not bring forth bad fruit. Then we will become an apostolic church again.

Part II:

The Journey

Chapter 5

THE

WILDERNESS

After the Red Sea experience, the Israelites were understandably elated. Without losing anything, they had just escaped from the most impossible of circumstances. There is no elation like that which comes when a great victory follows a seemingly hopeless situation. But few of them had even begun to understand the pattern of God's deliverances. They still did not understand that His greatest miracles are only seen when His people have come to the end of their own abilities. Their continued experience in the wilderness would teach them this lesson well.

The Opposite of What They Were Promised

The Lord promised Israel a land flowing with milk and honey. Yet in the first place He led them to, there was not even any water! This confused Israel as it continues to confuse many who follow the Lord today. Even so, this experience highlights one of the basic principles of our walk with God: *Between the place where we receive the promise of God and the Promised Land (the fulfillment of the promise), there is usually going to be a wilderness which is the exact opposite of what we have been promised.*

This principle is applicable to every promise of God, regardless of what it relates to: gifts, ministries, the salvation of loved ones, or even temporal things. In order for the promise to be fulfilled, there will be a barren place that requires faith between the place where we receive the promise and the attainment of the promise.

Abraham was promised a son. Though he was already too old when he was called, yet, before the promised son came, he had to wait through many more years of barrenness until conception for him and Sarah was *completely impossible* in the natural. The greatest promises of God will require the most faith and patience on our part.

Abraham's descendants were promised an inheritance in Canaan that flowed with milk and honey, but they had to spend four hundred years in Egypt as slaves before they received it. By the time they received it there could be no doubt that God was their Provider. They would also have a profound appreciation for what they had received.

Joseph was given a dream that even the sun, moon and stars would bow to him, but first he had to become a slave!

Though he had been a prince, Moses spent forty years in the desert as a shepherd, the most humble profession of his time, before he was ready to lead God's people. After David was anointed king, he spent years fleeing from the very people he was to rule over. They would actually try to kill him before they would submit to him. The church was promised that it would rule and reign with Christ over the earth, but it has for nearly two thousand years been *ruled by* the world that it is one day to have dominion over.

The purpose of this process can be summed up in one word: PREPARATION. Israel's experience in the wilderness was a time of preparation for the formation and maturing of their faith. Even more importantly, it was in the wilderness that Israel was to build a habitation for God so that He might dwell among them. This biblical process remains the same for us today. It is in our wilderness experiences that we too learn to make a habitation for God in our own lives.

After his dramatic conversion, the apostle Paul went into the wilderness for a number of years. He later wrote to the Galatians (1:11-17) that it was when the Father had revealed His Son *in* him (not just *to* him) that he was ready to preach.

It is in the wilderness that we come to abide in the Lord and He in us. Like Israel, we may enter the gateway to the Promised Land with all the treasures of Egypt, but we will have to learn to depend on the Lord for even a drink of water. It is in the wilderness that He is made our Lord and we become His priests. It is there that we become intimate with

Him and learn His ways. There the facades of our old nature are stripped away, and we come to know how desperately we need the transformation He is working in us.

The wilderness will contain our greatest difficulties, but also some of our most glorious experiences. We must know thirst before we will seek water from the Rock. We must be hungry before we taste the Manna from heaven.

Every great trial in the wilderness is followed by the most wonderful revelations of the King and His salvation. The wilderness is not a curse; it is a blessing. It is a place where the world's grip on our hearts and minds is loosened and we are captivated by the Lord and His eternal purposes. It is the place where the carnal nature's dominance is broken and the Lord begins to rule in our lives.

Turning Bitter Waters into Sweet

God's promise to Israel was clear that He would bring them to **"a land flowing with milk and honey" (Exodus 3:8).** Then, for the first three days of their journey toward that land, they did not even have water to drink. Try to comprehend how great this trial was. Have you ever gone without any liquids for just one day? Think what it would be like for *three* days, which takes a person to the very limits of what the human body can endure. Then think about doing this in the wilderness with two million people kicking dust in your face! This was a trial!

Naturally, they began to complain. Their basic instinct to survive was probably aroused as never before. Then, when they finally came to a well and their hopes rose to the very heights, the waters were bitter! There are probably few human beings who have ever comprehended this kind of disappointment. However, this is the first lesson we must learn in the wilderness—*how to turn bitter waters into sweet waters.*

Though the Israelites may have had a reason to complain, this difficult test was also their greatest opportunity. Real tests bring forth real faith. True faith is internal, not external. It is not dependent upon external circumstances. True faith is not altered by disappointment, but is instead strengthened by it. True faith will always turn the bitter waters of disappointment into the sweet waters of opportunity. True faith will always look into the greatest disappointments to find the treasure that God is providing for them in it. And God has always provided such a treasure for those who believe in Him.

Because Israel did not react to their trials of disappointment with faith, but rather with complaining, the destroyer was often released among them. When disappointment results in complaining, the destroyer of our faith has been released, and much will be lost. The wilderness is meant to test our faith, and we must learn to seize every opportunity to grow from the experiences there. *DON'T WASTE YOUR TRIALS!*

The Language of Unbelief

Even though we gain so much from our wilderness experiences, it is not God's intention that we stay there any longer than necessary. The distance from the point where Israel departed Egypt to Kadesh-Barnea, the place where the Lord originally intended that they enter the Promised Land, is only a ten to fourteen day journey by foot.

They were not going to get out of the wilderness quite that fast, as they first had to receive the Lord's covenant through the Law and build the tabernacle so that the Lord could dwell among them. Even so, Israel was ready to enter the Promised Land about two years after they left Egypt. However, their lack of faith, demonstrated by their grumbling and complaining, resulted in a forty-year wait and the death of an entire generation before they could enter in.

Unfortunately, most Christians have repeated this same pattern. Because of their unbelief, they end up wandering in spiritual circles in the wilderness over and over until they perish there, never having truly or fully lived in the promises God gave them. Paul explained this to the Corinthians:

> **For I do not want you to be unaware, brethren, that our fathers were all under the cloud, and all passed through the sea;**
>
> **and all were baptized into Moses in the cloud and in the sea;**
>
> **and all ate the same spiritual food;**

and all drank the same spiritual drink, for they were drinking from a spiritual rock which followed them; and the rock was Christ.

Nevertheless, WITH MOST OF THEM *God was not well-pleased*; **for they were laid low in the wilderness (I Corinthians 10:1-5).**

This is not to conclude that those who failed to enter the Promised Land were eternally condemned. As a type, they had experienced the salvation of the cross through the Passover. They were baptized into Christ at the Red Sea. They had even become His priests and ministers. But they still did not enter the Promised Land.

There is far more to our purpose in God than just being "saved." He has a Promised Land for us that we must possess. The Lord did not call Israel out of Egypt only to deliver them from bondage. His purpose was to use them as the vehicle of His redemption so that the whole world could be delivered from her bondage.

Certainly it was better for them to have perished in the wilderness than to have never left Egypt. They did, at least, begin to walk with God, but the first generation to leave Egypt did not continue in faith so as to fulfill their purpose. Most Christians do the same thing. Having left the world, they wander in circles in the place between the world and the Promised Land. They never conquer the strongholds which are keeping them from possessing God's promises to them.

We have not been called to perish in the wilderness! The desert is not our home. The Lord does not want us to stay there any longer than we have to. We were called out of Egypt to go to the Promised Land.

The first generation to leave Egypt did not enter their inheritance because of unbelief, which was displayed by their constant grumbling and complaining. Complaining is a telltale sign of a hardened, unbelieving heart. Complaining can cause major problems, each of which is deadly. First it destroys our own faith. Then it destroys the faith of those who hear us. Finally, instead of resulting in the reprieve from God that we are seeking, constant murmuring and complaining kindles His anger.

As the writer of Hebrews warned:

Therefore, just as the Holy Spirit says,

"Today if you hear His voice,

Do not harden your hearts as when they provoked Me,

As in the day of trial in the wilderness,

Where your fathers tried Me by testing Me, and saw My works for forty years.

"Therefore I was angry with this generation,

And said, 'They always go astray in their heart;

And they did not know My ways';

As I swore in My wrath,

'They shall not enter My rest.'"

Take care, brethren, lest there should be in any one of you an evil, unbelieving heart, in falling away from the living God.

BUT ENCOURAGE ONE ANOTHER day after day (Hebrews 3:7-13).

Faith moves God. Unbelief provokes Him and will never result in our deliverance. Faith is the straightest path to the fulfillment of the promises. Unbelief is the path to a never-ending circle in the desert. We will not attain the promises of God with it in our heart.

Complaining is the language of unbelief. Praise is the language of faith. The wilderness is the place where the Lord makes His habitation in us and He inhabits the praises of His people (Psalm 22:3 KJV). The praise God inhabits is more than just repeated accolades; it is a rejoicing, believing heart which proves itself as true praise when it prevails through even the most difficult circumstances.

The Lord has ordained that we pass through the wilderness to get to the Promised Land because it is in the wilderness that the truly faithful are separated from the false. No pretender will attain the Lord's promises. Even so, there are few who are truly faithful at the beginning of the journey. In the wilderness, though, many who began faithless do become faithful, or full of faith. That is His purpose for the wilderness. When we come to understand this, we will be able to say with James:

Consider it all joy, my brethren, when you encounter various trials,

knowing that the testing of your faith produces endurance.

And let endurance have its perfect result, that you may be perfect and complete, lacking in nothing (James 1:2-4).

Chapter 6

Turning Trials into Treasure

The separation of pretentious faith from true faith is just the beginning of God's purpose for the wilderness. After separation comes purification. If we want to know the truth, we must first be made true. If we want to see the glory, we must be cleansed to receive it. Pain and suffering do not cleanse, but the faith required to endure and persevere does.

True faith is simply the recognition of the One in Whom we believe. The more clearly that we see Him, the more pure our faith will be. The trying and purifying of our faith is more precious than anything we could ever carry out of Egypt. This purification enables us to see the Lord more clearly and to dwell in His presence.

> Now the Lord is the Spirit; and where the Spirit of the Lord is, there is liberty.
>
> But we all, with unveiled face beholding as in a mirror the glory of the Lord, are being transformed into the same image from glory to glory, just as from the Lord, the Spirit (II Corinthians 3:17-18).

To see His glory and be changed into His image, the veils must be stripped away. That is the purpose of the wilderness.

One of my favorite preachers used to begin his salvation messages with "Come to Jesus and He will wreck your life!" The Christian walk is meant to be a difficult one. Some try to manipulate people into making "decisions" for the Lord. They try to entice with the hope of prosperity if the sinner will just "accept Jesus." Yet when men came to the real Jesus, they were compelled to give up what they had. It is only after this that we will be able to handle the great prosperity of the Promised Land.

What God has promised greatly exceeds what the limited human mind can comprehend. But the reason so few who make "decisions" for the Lord are faithful to them is because we fail to explain that there is a wilderness to go through before we can enter into the promises.

The children of Israel had all the treasure of Egypt with them in the wilderness. They just did not have any place to spend it! The church also is the heir of the Owner of the universe, but to date we have been able to only cash a few small checks on His account. The reason for this is explained in Galatians 4:1-7:

> **Now I say, as long as the heir is a child, he does not differ at all from a slave although he is owner of everything,**
>
> **but he is under guardians and managers until the date set by the father.**
>
> **So also we, while we were children, were held in bondage under the elemental things of the world.**
>
> **But when the fulness of the time came, God sent forth His Son, born of a woman, born under the Law,**
>
> **in order that He might redeem those who were under the Law, that we might receive the adoption as sons.**
>
> **And because you are sons, God has sent forth the Spirit of His Son into our hearts, crying, "Abba! Father!"**
>
> **Therefore you are no longer a slave, but a son; and if a son, then an heir through God.**

Christians are the true nobility. Every Christian that has been born again is born from the seed of God. We are not the heirs of an earthly king, but of the King of Kings. All of the wealth on the earth could not compare to the inheritance of even the least of the saints of God. Even so, we are not called to a life of ease, comfort and luxury. As true knights of the Holy Spirit, we are called to a life of sacrifice and warfare. In this sacrifice and warfare we are promised unspeakable joy and peace in our heart. This is far more valuable than earthly riches, but even that is not the focus of our purpose. We are called to become free so that we can set the rest of the world's captives free.

Dietrich Bonhoeffer, the famous German theologian who was martyred in one of Hitler's concentration camps, once declared: "When Jesus calls a man, He bids him to come and die." When Jesus called men to follow Him, He specified that the sacrifice and commitment required was *total*. Those who preach any other gospel may be destroying more than they are saving.

One of the primary purposes of the Lord's ministry on earth was to aid the needy and oppressed. However, He did not call men to follow Him on that basis. The gospel does inherently declare freedom and deliverance, peace and fulfillment. All of these things are free but none of them are cheap. The true gospel declares emphatically that **"Whoever wishes to save his life shall lose it; but whoever loses his life for My sake shall find it" (Matthew 16:25).**

The ones who respond to a gospel of cheap grace inevitably perish in the wilderness or return to "Egypt." Those who respond to the true calling of Christ will have difficult times. The Lord never said His way would be easy. He only said it would be worth it. There is only one path to the Promised Land, and it leads through the wilderness.

However, our ultimate goal must be for much more than just getting to the Promised Land ourselves. **"The Son of God appeared for this purpose, that He might destroy the works of the devil" (I John 3:8).** He prayed on that last night before

His passion, **"As Thou didst send Me into the world, I also have sent them into the world" (John 17:18).** We too have been sent to destroy the works of the devil. As John also wrote, **"The whole world lies in the power of the evil one" (I John 5:19).** We are here to take it back. Our inheritance is in Christ, and His inheritance is clearly stated in Psalm 2:7-8:

> **"I will surely tell of the decree of the LORD:**
> **He said to Me, 'Thou art My Son,**
> **Today I have begotten Thee.**
> **'Ask of Me, and I will surely give the nations as**
> **Thine inheritance,**
> **And the very ends of the earth as Thy possession.'"**

God entrusted authority over the entire earth to Adam. When Adam submitted himself to the seduction of the serpent, he became the slave of the one he obeyed. The entire world came under the dominion of Satan. The enemy has carefully ordered his domain to make it as hard as possible for men to return to God and submit themselves back to Him.

Satan is too subtle to manifest himself so that we would worship him directly. He continues to come as he did in the serpent; he gets us to worship him by conforming to his ways. Knowing that it takes faith and patience to follow God and to inherit His promises, Satan has constructed the systems of the modern world to feed both our doubt and our impatience.

The Scriptures testify repeatedly that it was God's plan before the foundation of the world to bring many sons to glory. This was His intention regardless of the fall of man.

Had man not fallen, God still intended for him to mature to the place in his relationship with God that he would bridge the chasm between the spiritual and natural worlds as a truly new creation.

God always intended for man to mature to the place where he comprehended His ways and His wisdom. Because of man's fall, the whole plan of redemption was added. Redemption was God's plan to bring man back to the place from which he had fallen. Until the world is redeemed, that aspect of God's plan will continue to work; therefore we must continue to preach redemption. Even so, we must not lose sight of God's ultimate purpose for man. Man was not just to be made in the image of God, but he was also to become like God in nature and spirit.

Satan actually tempted man with the ultimate purpose of God. God has repeatedly stated that He really does want us to be like Him. Satan tempted man into trying to take an easier, shorter way to this objective. The fall came when man was deceived into thinking there could be an easier and quicker way to get there—*just eat this fruit!*

God's purpose for man was not changed because of the fall. The plan of redemption is simply a part of God's ultimate purpose for man, to be conformed fully to the image of His Son. The plan of salvation is not the whole plan of God—it is a modification required because of the fall. God's ultimate goal for us is that we **"attain to the unity of the faith, and of the knowledge of the Son of God, to a mature man, *to the***

measure of the stature which belongs to the fulness of Christ"
(Ephesians 4:13).

To lose sight of the ultimate purpose of God is to fall short and die in the wilderness. After our baptism and commitment to live for the Lord and not for ourselves, the wilderness is there to make this commitment a reality. The wilderness is meant to be tough. But the fruit of our experience is a faith that is tougher than anything the world can throw at us. After the wilderness, we will be dead to the world, but alive to God.

After the wilderness, we will have His presence with us, a treasure far more valuable than anything the world has to offer. The Promised Land will be wonderful, but nothing can be as wonderful as having the Lord make us His dwelling place. The wilderness will not be easy, but the fruit will be worth everything we have to go through.

Chapter 7

FAITH

AND

PATIENCE

We are exhorted to **"not be sluggish, but imitators of those who through faith and patience inherit the promises"** (Hebrews 6:12). Should we then be surprised or discouraged when, after receiving a promise from the Lord, its fulfillment starts to seem increasingly remote? It was said of Abraham, "the father of faith," that **"having *patiently* waited, he obtained the promise"** (Hebrews 6:15).

Patience is the demonstration of faith, yet few comprehend this. Because of the failure to understand this, few go on to attain their promises or fulfill their callings. Approximately two million Israelites left Egypt, but only two men from that generation entered the Promised Land. That is one in a million.

Does that discourage you? If it does, it is a call to believe God. It is a call to become a Joshua or Caleb who, in spite of seeing the same giants in the land that caused other leaders to quake in fear, determined to believe God. It is better to die believing God than to live in unbelief.

The second generation that was raised in the wilderness comprehended this lesson because they spent forty years watching their fathers perish by their unbelief. That whole generation did cross over and enter the Promised Land. We too can enter if we but learn from the failures of the generations who have gone before us. We do not have to perish in the wilderness. We must not be content to wander in circles. We have the testimony of God's dealings with men. We can understand His ways because of the biblical accounts of those who have walked with Him.

Paul recounted the ways of God with Israel in the wilderness so that those who heard them could be instructed by them:

> **These things happened as examples for us, that we should not crave evil things, as they also craved.**
>
> **And do not be idolaters, as some of them were; as it is written, "The people sat down to eat and drink, and stood up to play."**
>
> **Nor let us act immorally, as some of them did, and twenty-three thousand fell in one day.**
>
> **Nor let us try the Lord, as some of them did, and were destroyed by the serpents.**

> **Nor grumble, as some of them did, and were destroyed by the destroyer.**
>
> *Now these things happened to them as an example, and they were written for OUR INSTRUCTION, upon whom the ends of the ages have come.*
>
> **Therefore let him who thinks he stands take heed lest he fall (I Corinthians 10:6-12).**

The Lord's dealings with men have been consistent from the patriarchs right through until today. We have an even more comprehensive testimony of His ways than the first-century church because we also have the history of the church from that time. Like Moses, we must concern ourselves more with knowing His ways. We must not be satisfied with just witnessing His acts.

Mount Sinai

Soon after entering the wilderness, Israel was to experience what may have been her most difficult trial— waiting! Moses left the people alone so that he could go up on the mountain to receive the Ten Commandments. We too must pass this same test in each wilderness we are called to cross. Going for a period of time without feeling the nearness of the Lord is the most difficult test of all.

The first couple of weeks after Moses went up the mountain were probably not too difficult. After a few more weeks, however, they started to wonder what had happened to him. Before long, they were convinced that he was not going to ever come back down. So they started making plans to live without him.

This is typical of one of the most serious tests we must all endure as we go through the wilderness. To be given nothing to do but wait can be the most difficult trial we ever have to endure. When our Deliverer seems to have left us, even the mighty miracles we have witnessed become vague in our memory after awhile. Then the doubts come sweeping in. Are we out of His will? Did He move on without us? Have I sinned so that He departed from me? Ad infinitum.

Of course, the answer is "no" to all of these doubts. But reason will seldom be of comfort in that place of seeming abandonment by God. We want Him. We start to feel like He is never coming back. Just before Moses' appearance, they could stand it no longer. They turned back to their old ways. If they could have just held out for a few more days!

It is often the same with us. We usually give in to our doubts and fears at the very end of the test. We fall just before our Deliverer appears. We usually lose this battle when we are on the very threshold of victory. It takes faith *and* patience to inherit the promises (Hebrews 6:12). It is usually our patience that starts failing first and causes us to compromise our faith.

For you have need of endurance, so that when you have done the will of God, you may receive what was promised (Hebrews 10:36).

He endured, as seeing Him who is unseen (Hebrews 11:27).

Israel's lack of endurance was costly. So is ours. Not only did thousands perish from the impending judgment (Exodus 32), but those who remained had to begin the trial all over again (Exodus 34). This test of endurance causes many to perish in their faith and cease to follow the Lord. Those who repent and desire to follow the Lord must endure the test again. We will not go on until we have learned to wait upon the Lord. Impatience is so deadly that the Lord will not trust us with the blessing of the Promised Land until we have been delivered from it.

We usually give up just before the victory—just before our Lord appears with His covenant for us carved in stone. If He does not find us waiting, then the covenant is broken. When He left, He commanded us to wait for His return. He is coming back, but not until the work in us has been completed.

When we get to the place where we do not think that we can stand another day, we should start rejoicing because His return is near. He has promised us that He would not allow us to be tempted beyond what we are able to endure (I Corinthians 10:13). Waiting is one of the great tests of the saints. Every patriarch had to endure it to receive the promises, and we will be no different.

Patience is faith. Impatience is the very tap root of self-will. The lack of patience caused the first sin and has caused most of the sin and corruption since. It is impossible to walk with God without patience. It is required to receive His promises. Impatience caused the breaking of the first covenant, and it will cause the breaking of the new one as well. This test is essential and is rightly placed at the beginning of our journey. Many do perish in their faith here. The rest learn patience. This was the first great separation required to determine those who would follow the Lord fully.

It is not without purpose that there are so many Scriptures exhorting us to wait upon the Lord. There are no Scriptures which encourage us to hurry. C.J. Jung once stated, "Hurry is not of the devil, it *is* the devil!" This is not far from the truth. The devil no doubt gets into more projects, even those that are ordained by God, because of our impatience than for any other reason. In contrast, the Lord exudes patience in all that He does.

Having been a jet pilot, I know about speed. Speed is addictive. The faster you go, the less satisfied you are with the speed you are going. You just want to keep going faster. I've looked down on the contrails of commercial jets and passed them by. But that wasn't enough for me. I've gotten more impatient when I'm going somewhere at over 500 miles per hour than when I'm walking. People often get more impatient waiting in a short line at a fast food restaurant than they do waiting for a meal in a fine restaurant.

We can't stand to wait. We can't stand to go slow. But to get to the Promised Land we must learn to both wait and to go slow. We will cover a lot more ground in the wilderness by going fast, but it will be the *same ground* because we will be going in circles. In almost everything done through impatience, we spend more time undoing and redoing than doing.

Chapter 8

The Foundation of Faith

When Abraham was called to follow the Lord, he was required to leave all that he had ever known, in order to wander in a wilderness seeking a place that he had never seen. Babylon was one of the great wonders of the world. It had buildings, gardens, magnificent streets and homes, science, culture and one of the world's most powerful armies. To be a citizen of Babylon was to be the envy of the world. To be an heir of one of its leading families and to leave it all to wander about in a wilderness for a mere dream was incomprehensible!

Abraham's relatives and friends probably considered him either foolish, irresponsible or insane. But the dream was more important to Abraham than anything the world could offer. What Abraham saw with the eyes of his heart was more real to him than what he saw with his physical eyes. Such was the constitution of the man who became "the father of faith." Such is the nature of true faith. True faith is of the heart, not of the mind.

The eyes of faith see what others cannot see. Those who have faith live by a different standard. Those who can perceive eternity with their hearts will pay any price and make any sacrifice to be a part of the city that God is building. Eternity makes a vapor out of all the world's riches and pleasures. Once eternity is in our hearts, faith is galvanized. Then our trials become treasures, as they are seen as discipline that will help us to attain fruit that will last forever.

The earthly-minded refer to those like Abraham as being "too heavenly minded to be any earthly good." The truth is that most Christians are probably too earthly-minded to do any good spiritually. Vision is the foundation of faith. Those with vision will be "heavenly-minded." Once we have a taste of the glories and power of the age to come, we simply cannot be too interested in things that are earthly.

There can be no faith without spiritual vision. We have faith to the degree that we have vision. To the spiritual man, a vision will have more substance than all of the world's treasures and pleasures. Although spiritual vision will always appear as foolishness to everyone who does not have it, what is seen with the eyes of faith is far more real than anything that can be seen with our physical eyes.

Babylon, despite all its splendor, wealth and power, no longer exists. It was but a vapor, a wisp of smoke quickly blown away by the changing winds of time. But Abraham stands forever as one of the greatest men who ever walked upon the earth. He loved God. He desired God and His habitation more than the best the world could give.

The Price of Admission

There is a great cost to walking in spiritual vision. Each of us must leave our Babylon, our Egypt. In some cases, as it was with David, we may even be cut off from the people of God for a season. The ways of the world, and of those who put their hope in it, are contrary to the ways of the Spirit. Those who follow the Spirit will inevitably be misunderstood and persecuted by those who are earthly-minded.

Immediately following Abraham's great demonstration of faith, leaving both his city and his family to strike out into a wilderness, one might have expected God to quickly give him all that he sought. That was not the case. The trials and waiting required of Abraham were long and difficult, beyond the ability of many to even comprehend, much less endure.

The main vision that Abraham had when he left his home, that of living in the City of God, he did not attain on earth. He only saw it from afar. But that was enough for Abraham. He attained it in his heart, and knowing eternity, he did not care about receiving it here in the temporary realm.

What Abraham saw with the eyes of his heart and received was more real to him than anything he could have received here. For him to have been given the greatest earthly cities to rule would probably have been profoundly boring to him. Even so, he was a prince in the earth as well. He became one of the greatest men in the earthly realm as well, though he probably did not care about it, and may not have even been aware of it. Those who walk with such spiritual vision usually press so far beyond the limits of their times that they do have a great impact on earth, but being known on earth is not their goal—being known in heaven is.

When you see by the Spirit, you see beyond time. When we begin to see by the Spirit, we begin to live in eternity. Each of us lives in the realm that we see most clearly. It did not matter to Abraham whether he lived in a tent or a palace, because he knew that his true dwelling place was the City of God.

Abraham recognized that his time on earth, Babylon, even his beloved son Isaac—all these were only wisps of smoke that appear for a little while and then vanish away. He saw eternity and fastened the grip of his soul upon it. When we, like Abraham, begin to abide in eternity, patience will become our nature. It is hard to get in a hurry when you have forever.

Turning Stumbling Blocks into Stepping Stones

Abraham did have failures. He drifted from the reality of his vision at times, as we are all prone to do. He made mistakes and occasionally slipped. Yet his vision had enough substance to draw him right back to the course. Some of the greatest men of God have made some of the greatest mistakes. Getting back on the course and continuing after our mistakes sometimes requires the greatest faith of all. It is usually after our failures that we come to the reality that our greatest efforts cannot attain our goal. It is here that our faith becomes true. At this point it becomes directed more at the One who is Truth. Our faith must be in Him, not in ourselves and not even in our faith.

Our pretenses of righteousness and our delusions of success gained by our own efforts are stripped away by failures. Here we come to understand the crucial truth that the only work which we can do for God is to believe in Him. Everything that we have received, we have received *from Him*—even our faith.

Therefore, even though those who have true faith may get knocked down occasionally, they will always get back up and be stronger than ever, regardless of how detestable their mistakes may have been. Most of the heroes of Scripture rose to their greatest victories after their worst mistakes. God is in the redemption business, and He testifies of this through the life of everyone He calls.

The Temptation

One of Abraham's greatest mistakes was giving in to his wife Sarah's suggestion to use Hagar, her slave, to bring forth the promised son. When the Lord gives us a promise and we have waited a long time without seeing it fulfilled, we will likely be subject to this same temptation.

It is then easy to rationalize trying to bring forth the promise of God by our own devices. Most of us, like Abraham, succumb to it at least once. At the time, our actions may seem like the Lord's provision. But while it seems reasonable that we should give the Lord a little help, the consequences of this delusion can be devastating. Ishmael seemed to Abraham like the promised seed, until the true seed was born.

When Ishmael was born, the angel of the Lord prophesied that he would be **"a wild donkey of a man, his hand will be against everyone, and everyone's hand will be against him" (Genesis 16:12).** Our wild ideas will bring forth wild results. To this day, the sons of Ishmael, the Arabs, are against everyone and everyone is against them. The failure to wait upon God to bring about what He promises will always result in major problems.

Soon the enmity between the one born after the flesh and the one born after the Spirit became apparent. Before Isaac was weaned, Ishmael was mocking him. Finally, Abraham had to drive Ishmael away. That did not end the conflict, though; Ishmael's descendants continue to persecute the descendants of Isaac, the Jews, to this day. Likewise, when we attempt to bring forth God's promise by our own efforts, we can create problems that follow us for the rest of our lives and even affect our descendants.

Because he was the son of His friend, God loved and blessed Ishmael. He still loves and blesses the sons of Ishmael as much as He can. The Scriptures testify that there will be a great harvest among the Arab peoples, and ultimately a great unity between them and Israel. But blessings are not the same as inheritance.

The Lord also will often bless our spiritual Ishmaels. Because of this, many never realize that the true seed has not yet been born. There are many large ministries and churches that reach and bless multitudes, but are in fact spiritual Ishmaels born after the flesh. In most cases the leaders had a true calling to the work. However, very few are able to wait for God's best, in His timing. These "Ishmaels" are easily discerned. Ishmael is of the earthly seed, born after the flesh, and they can only be sustained with striving and toil.

We must not mistake the blessing of the Lord for the *presence* of the Lord. When the true seed appears, there will always be great conflict. The Ishmaels will try to destroy the Isaacs who have come to take their place. Those who follow after appearances will almost certainly follow Ishmael. God's chosen seed, whether it is a work or a person, seldom appears to the earthly- minded to be of much good.

Even the appearance of Jesus was such that none would be attracted to Him in the natural (Isaiah 53:2). The only way that the Messiah could be recognized was by the Spirit. The true seed will appear to the earthly-minded as insignificant. Even the foremost of the apostles, Paul, came in **"weakness**

and in fear and in much trembling" (I Corinthians 2:3). Those prone to judge by appearances will embrace the carnal seed and scorn the true seed.

When we have perceived the Lord, all the pomp and glory of the world appears ludicrous and profane. When we have "seen" the City of God, the greatest works of man are trivial. Whether we live in a castle or a cave, if we are abiding in the Lord we abide in glory.

This is the faith of Abraham—to keep going forward until we *see the Lord and live with our hearts fastened to eternity.* True faith comes by having the Lord open "the eyes of our hearts" until we see Him and His city more clearly than we see this present world. In the process, we will begin to treasure our time in the wilderness, because it is there that we become more intimate with Him. There we will build His habitation that He might dwell among us. In the wilderness, even though we may trod years through dry places, all the treasures of Egypt or Babylon will lose their significance as we perceive the treasures of Christ.

Chapter 9

Promises Fulfilled and Lost

Isaac was the long-awaited promised son. He bore the nature of the holy seed. As a type of Christ, there are many parallels in Isaac's life that testify of the Lord Jesus. Isaac patiently bore the wood for his own sacrifice. He submitted without resistance. After the sacrifice, he patiently waited for his father to provide him with a bride, just as Jesus is patiently waiting for the completion of His bride. Isaac loved Rebecca "as he loved himself" as a testimony of how Jesus would love His church.

God's command to sacrifice Isaac was certainly one of Abraham's greatest trials, just as the greatest statement of our heavenly Father's love was His willingness to sacrifice His Son for us. Abraham had already "sacrificed" his beloved Ishmael for Isaac. Now he would not only be deprived of both sons, but that would seem to certainly deprive him of the promise of God!

Abraham had waited so long and been through so much for Isaac. Yet, after giving Isaac to Abraham and Sarah, God required that Isaac be sacrificed. It is hard to comprehend how difficult this would have been. It was to be through Isaac that all nations of the earth were to be blessed. If he was sacrificed, how could this promise of God be fulfilled?

Even after we prove willing to leave all that Babylon has to offer, spend years as a sojourner in the wilderness until we finally attain the promise, realize our mistakes and drive out our Ishmaels, there is yet one major test. Are we willing to lay our promised one on the altar? Are we willing to give everything back into the hands of God? This too will be required of us.

After having gone through so much to attain them, it is easy for the promises of God to take precedence over God Himself. When they do, they have become idols. We must never become so attached to the work of God that we forget the God of the work. Probably the most pervasive idolatry in the church is the worship of the things of God.

Our idols may be a ministry, a truth, or even the church. We may even worship our worship in place of worshiping God Himself. The greatest danger for this to happen occurs after we have waited for so long and endured so much to receive what was promised. For our sake, God requires that all promises received must pass this test.

Those who walk with God must always be willing to give up everything but Him. Even our "Isaacs" will be required of us. If we lose everything but Him, we will then know for sure that He is enough. He is all we ever really need.

Soon after Abraham proved willing to sacrifice Isaac, Sarah died. Her death, like her life, is a message. Israel was metaphorically the Father's bride. The fruit of their relationship would bring forth the Messiah. After Sarah died, Isaac was able to take a bride. After the sacrifice of Jesus, His "mother," Israel, died spiritually. Jesus, the Son, then took His own bride—the church.

Rebecca brought forth two sons by Isaac. The Lord told her there were "two nations" that would come forth from her, represented by these two sons. These two nations are a continuation of the two seeds that came forth from the first woman. Even through the church, the bride of Christ, two seeds are going to emerge: one carnal like Cain, "a tiller of the ground," or earthly-minded; the other spiritual, coming to God on the basis of the blood sacrifice. There is destined to be both a carnal and a spiritual church. The carnal church continues to persecute the true church, just as the carnal seed has persecuted the spiritual seed from the beginning.

Famines and the Seed of Promise

It is significant that a famine occurred during the life of each of the patriarchs, Abraham, Isaac and Jacob. All three were dwelling in the Promised Land when the droughts came which caused the famines. All three turned to Egypt, a type of the world, for sustenance during the famine (Isaac was prevented by the Lord from actually reaching Egypt, though he was headed there).

Unfortunately, this has been a historic principle even for the promised, spiritual seed. When there is a famine in the land, our first inclination is to turn to Egypt (the world) for our provision. In Egypt, Abraham became a liar and deceiver; he even compromised his wife. Jacob actually led the family of promise into slavery for four hundred years.

Even when we are dwelling in the promises of God there will be times of dryness, and even famine. These are allowed for a purpose. Every test is meant to draw us closer to the Lord. They are opportunities to grow in faith and walk in higher levels of obedience. They are also potential stumbling blocks. If we turn to the world for our provision during those times, our degradation will be swift. The patriarchs were all restored to the land, but their sojourn in Egypt was costly.

When we are enduring the discipline of God, it will always cost us if we turn back to the world for help. Even when we have attained the promises of God, we cannot let down our guard. At the time when we begin to walk in the fulfillment of what He has called us to, we are still in a vulnerable place. When a believer begins to walk in the provision of God, he may be in the greatest danger of forgetting who the Provider is. Moses warned Israel of this just before they were to enter the Promised Land:

> **Then it shall come about when the LORD your God brings you into the land which He swore to your fathers, Abraham, Isaac and Jacob, to give you great and splendid cities which you did not build,**
>
> **and houses full of all good things which you did not fill, and hewn cisterns which you did not dig, vineyards and olive trees which you did not plant, and you shall eat and be satisfied,**
>
> **THEN WATCH YOURSELF, lest you forget the LORD who brought you from the land of Egypt (Deuteronomy 6:10-12).**

When the trials and battles are intense we are usually quick to seek the Lord. When we begin to walk in the promises and everything is going well, we do have the tendency to become complacent, often slipping into compromise. Then, when the famine comes, our hearts are already inclined in the wrong direction, and we turn to the ways of the world for our provision.

In this age, there is no time or place that we can let down our guard or refrain from drawing near to the Lord. In fact, when things go well we may be in the most dangerous place of all. There is a reason for the trials and dry times in the wilderness. They bring us back to a place of continual dependency and intimacy with the Lord. Then the blessings of the Promised Land will not be our undoing. It requires great maturity to safely dwell in the promises of God. If the Lord Himself has not become more important than the blessings, then the blessings themselves can easily become our downfall.

It is the Lord who allows dry times and, if necessary, even famines—*in the Promised Land*. They come to wake us up, not to trip us up. However, if we do not awaken from our complacency we will stumble. There have been countless churches and individuals that have attained and walked in the promises that were given to them, only to fall again into bondage and degradation. Many great men of God have fallen right at the very end of their lives, just before their graduation into glory. As Moses warned, when you begin to walk in what you were called to achieve, THEN WATCH YOURSELF! Even when we know His rest and know His peace, we must not become complacent and lay down our defenses.

Like Abraham before him and Jacob after him, when famine came in the days of Isaac, he started to go to Egypt. God prevented him from going to Egypt, and told him to stay in the land that He had promised (Genesis 26:1-5). But Isaac drifted and ended up staying in Gerar of the Philistines (verse 6). He did not go all the way down to Egypt; he just went part of the way.

This is typical of what many of us try to do. As Egypt is typical of the present evil age, the Philistines represent the flesh in Scripture. Every time "those uncircumcised" are spoken of in the Old Testament, it is in relation to the Philistines. Circumcision was typical of the cutting away of the excessive flesh in our life. Though Isaac may not have returned all the way to the world, he drifted into the place of carnality.

It is significant that Isaac dwelt in Gerar, a place whose name literally means "circle." This is where we find ourselves if we go even part of the way back to Egypt—going in circles. When we are not quite in the world, but we are not abiding in the Promised Land either, we will be in confusion.

It probably confused Isaac further that the Lord greatly blessed him while he was in Gerar (verses 12-14). The gifts and callings of God are irrevocable (Romans 11:29). God is faithful to us even if we become unfaithful to Him. We must not mistake the blessings of the Lord for either His presence or His approval. It is a common but dangerous assumption to believe that blessings are in themselves evidence that a person is in the will of God.

One might wonder: If blessings are not necessarily a sign of being in God's will, then how can we know when we are in His will? The Lord Jesus testified that there are few who enter by this narrow way. Many miss the path that leads to life by taking the broad way. The realization that God's way is narrow and few endure to the end may causes us to feel insecure. The Lord *meant* for it to make us insecure in anything but Him, and we must even lose the security that we have in ourselves.

Our trials, with all the potential they bring for failure, are meant to bring us to a clinging dependency on the Lord. They are meant to instill a greater love for Him than for His blessings and a determination to know His ways and not just

His acts. Like the patriarchs, we may stumble many times, but those who are the true seed will always get back up and keep pressing on.

Isaac dug wells in Gerar and he found water. Yet each time he found water, the Philistines quarreled with him over it. We may even find water in these places of compromise, but it will not come with peace. The land of compromise is the land of contention and strife. Finally Isaac returned to Beersheba, which means "the place of the covenant," and the Lord appeared to him that same night (Genesis 26:23-24).

We will never know peace until we return to the place the Lord has called us to, the place of our original covenant with Him. As soon as we return to the place of our covenant, we will again see the Lord and find peace.

Chapter 10

THE TYRANNY OF THE FAMILIAR

The Passover delivered Israel from Egypt. The wilderness was meant to get the ways of Egypt out of Israel. It is the same for us. The Passover sacrifice of Jesus has delivered us from the power of the world. The trials we experience in our wilderness are meant to deliver us from the ways of the world that continue to dominate our thoughts and actions. We are redeemed by the blood of the Lamb, but we are also commanded to *"work out your salvation...for it is God who is at work in you"* **(Philippians 2:12-13).** Our wilderness experience is the place where this work takes place.

To derive the full benefit from our wilderness experiences, we must understand the nature of our spiritual bondage. It is the truth that sets us free. The wilderness is the place where we learn the truth about God and ourselves. One of the greatest yokes of bondage enslaving the human race is called "the tyranny of the familiar." It is the universal human temptation to cling to the familiar, regardless of how bad or painful it may be, and to resist change regardless of how promising it may be.

This is why, for example, a high percentage of children who have come from the homes of alcoholic parents are likely to marry heavy drinkers, regardless of the pain and turmoil they know that they can expect. The predictability of the familiar, even with the potential pain, is more desirable than the unknown which offers much greater peace and fulfillment. The "bondage to the familiar" is stronger than reason.

It was this bondage to the familiar that made Israel say to Moses: **"Would that we had died by the LORD'S hand in the land of Egypt, when we sat by the pots of meat, when we ate bread to the full" (Exodus 16:3).** Even though it was the hard oppression of slavery that caused them to call out to the Lord for deliverance, there was a kind of security in the slavery of Egypt that was more desirable to Israel than the unpredictability of following God.

In Egypt they at least knew what to expect. In the wilderness, where they had to trust God for their daily provision, they did not feel secure. Many in the church have been no less prone to endure the abuse, turmoil and pain of familiar circumstances that have them in bondage, rather than take the risk and be open to the change that inherently goes with following God.

The primary reason we are so prone to choose spiritual slavery over following God is our human tendency to put our security in our environment rather than in the Lord. Our inclination is to put our faith in circumstances which we can control or which will control us in a consistent and unchanging way that we can depend on.

With God we have the potential of much greater security and peace, but it must be in Him, not in our environment. The Lord does not change, but when we walk with Him we will pass through many changes in our environment. This is a very difficult yoke to break, and it is a primary purpose of our wilderness experience.

Submitting to Abuse

After the apostle Paul had made the sacrifice of laboring with his own hands so that he would not be a burden to the Corinthians, he marveled at how quickly they were carried away by false apostles who abused them. He wrote to them: **"For you bear with anyone if he enslaves you, if he devours you, if he takes advantage of you, if he exalts himself, if he hits you in the face" (II Corinthians 11:20).**

Consider the nature of the church authorities Paul describes here. He is speaking about ministers who had gained wide influence in the body of Christ. Paul was rebuking them for bearing with those who:

- enslaved them

- devoured or took advantage of them

- exalted themselves

- hit them in the face or humiliated them

Consider these characteristics in relation to the leadership that the body of Christ has been subject to throughout most of its history. How long will it take us to wake up? Regardless of their claims, those who do these things are false shepherds who have not been sent by God.

How could the Corinthians be so foolish as to follow such men? They did it for the same reason the church continues to do it today. They were deceived by their bondage to the familiar. The Corinthians were only familiar with the oppressive, self-serving nature of Roman authority. They were therefore prone to follow spiritual leaders who exhibited the familiar Roman style of leadership. The kind of leadership Jesus exhibited and requires of His true ministers was unfamiliar to them and challenged some of their misplaced security.

Carnal people respond to carnal authority. It takes a spiritual man to recognize and respond to true spiritual authority. *If we are going to walk in true spiritual authority, we must NOT allow anyone to enslave us, take advantage of us, exalt himself, or seek to control us through intimidation or humiliation.* Such leaders are false apostles, false prophets, false shepherds and false teachers.

We marvel at how the Israelites, after receiving manna from heaven and quail in abundance, could long for the **"flesh pots"** of Egypt (Exodus 16:3 KJV). Yet have we not done the same thing, over and over again? Church history is a continually repeating story of how the church chose the familiarity of spiritual slavery to the freedom of walking with God. This has caused the church to follow the ways of the world rather than the intentionally unpredictable wilderness that we must go through to get to the Promised Land. The history of the church is one of continual subjection to legalism and cruel spiritual taskmasters who have come exalting themselves.

The Ultimate Battle

The greatest conflict in the New Testament is the conflict between law and grace. Almost every book of the New Testament is both a fundamental statement of the liberty we have in Christ and a statement against the encroachment of legalism. When Jesus warned His disciples to **"beware of the leaven of the Pharisees" (Matthew 16:6 KJV),** He was talking about legalism.

This has been a continual battle since that time, and so far the battle has not been won. It may well be that the next movement that remains free of this leaven will be the very first one to do so. The one that does will likely find its way out of the wilderness into the Promised Land of God, making the way for the kingdom of God to come to the earth.

When we say that the church has continued to be subject to the law instead of walking in grace, this is not just talking about the Law of Moses. Legalism comes in many forms. We often think of the Old Testament as the law and the New Testament as grace, but that is not necessarily true. If we read the New Testament with an Old Covenant heart, it will just be law to us. Some of the laws we have wrested out of the New Testament often rival what the Pharisees did to the Old Testament.

A law squeezed out of the New Testament is just as much a yoke of legalism as those drawn from the Law of Moses. Because this issue of law and grace is addressed in depth in Volume I of this series—*There Were Two Trees in the Garden*— we will not belabor it further here. But we must keep in mind that this is the primary struggle. This conflict between law and grace is the very focal point of the conflict between the kingdom of God and this present evil age.

Fear is the door to Satan's domain and control, just as faith is the door to the kingdom of God. We submit ourselves to the control of that which we fear. No one wants to be deceived, but when we submit ourselves to the fear of error, in place of having a love for the truth, error will gain increasing dominion in our lives.

Some Christians, by submitting to the fear of error, now have more faith in Satan to deceive them than they have in the Lord to lead them into all truth. Thus the enemy is able to increase his control over their lives. Such Christians usually become so fearful of deception that they become increasingly isolated from the rest of the church, especially any groups that are not just like them. Ironically, this type of fear is the initial stage of those who end up as a sect or cult. Those who allow fear to control them are allowing Satan to have dominion in their life, even when it is a fear of error.

Many cult-watching ministries have helped to sound the alarm about the New Age and other deceptive movements. Yet, because they have sown a crippling paranoia with their teachings, many of these have actually done more damage than the New Age or the other deceptions they have tried to protect the church from. Others, leaving their true calling and commission in order to watch cults, have in effect usurped the work of the elders and shepherds by trying to be judges in the church. These almost inevitably go on to become stumbling blocks, publishing slander and hearsay as if it were researched fact, often showing even less integrity in their standards of research than the secular media.

The primary fruit of such ministries is to sow fear in the church that divides the body of Christ. Satan knows very well that **"any city or house divided against itself shall not stand" (Matthew 12:25).** Satan's number one strategy against the church is to bring division. The fruit of God's Spirit is love and faith that brings unity. The fruit of Satan's spirit sows suspicion and paranoia to bring division. Fear is a yoke of slavery, and those who lead with fear are false ministers.

Our God is a God of diversity. He makes every snow flake different. He makes every person different, every congregation different. If we would let Him, He would make every meeting and service unique. Why is it that the Lord continues to tell us that He is doing a "new thing?" Why is it that He continually does new things? The Lord works continual newness into church life to keep our faith in Him instead of in our environment. When God-ordained changes are upsetting to us, it is a revelation of how bound we are to the "tyranny of the familiar," and how little faith we really have in Him.

Wandering In Circles

Historically, there have been very few who have gone on to attain the promises of God. Most Christians do spend their lives wandering in circles in the wilderness. A primary reason for this is that few have been courageous enough to risk change, like Abraham, who was willing to strike out across unknown places to seek the city that God is building. When we understand the incredible power of our bondage to the familiar, we can only marvel at Abraham's extraordinary act of faith in leaving Ur of the Chaldees.

All who are of the true faith are called to do the deeds of Abraham. To truly walk with God we must be willing to leave the known to follow Him in unknown places. Each new spiritual generation has to make the choice between clinging to the familiar ways of the old order or being willing to go forth and seek God in new and unfamiliar places. Until we do this, there is little potential for true freedom in the Spirit and faith in God.

Only a few from each new generation or spiritual movement have been willing to depart from the multitudes, who cling to the security of the known, to follow the narrow path that is not often traveled. Indeed, on this path of faith are many dangers and possible deceptions, but this is the path that leads to the City of God.

Chapter 11

THE TYRANNY
OF CONFORMITY

The yoke of conformity is similar to the yoke of the familiar. This yoke is the result of our putting our security in men rather than in God. The biblical term for this yoke is "the fear of man." The pressure to conform to the crowd comes because we fear men more than we fear God.

True Christianity is in basic conflict with the ways of the world, which are usually the ways of the multitude. The yoke of conformity has been a primary reason why many fall away from the faith and succumb to the ways of the world. These desire the approval of men more than the approval of God.

Because of this yoke, Jesus sternly warned:

You are those who justify yourselves in the sight of men, but God knows your hearts; for that which is

highly esteemed among men is detestable in the sight of God (Luke 16:15).

This is a clear warning. If we do the things approved by men, we will be doing that which is detestable in the sight of God. The reverse is also true. The things that are approved by God are usually detestable in the sight of men. It is obvious that someone is going to detest what we do! Who do we want it to be—God or men?

There is a yoke that gives us freedom instead of bondage. The Lord's yoke is easy. When we take His yoke, we find rest for our souls instead of weariness. When we live by the pure and holy fear of God, we do not have to fear anything else on this earth. Solomon testified, **"The fear of man brings a snare" (Proverbs 29:25).** Those who are controlled by the fear of man and the pressure to conform can never find rest. They will always be in bondage to fears that can never be appeased or satisfied. However, when we have only One to please, we can find rest and peace like nothing else in the world can ever give to us.

When Israel did possess her Promised Land, she lived for a period of time with God as her King. She later chose to suffer bondage to an earthly monarch so that she could "be like the other nations." It was not that the rule of God was bad; it was just that His ways were sometimes unknown and His expectations mysterious. It is easier to put our security in men we can see, than in God who is unseen.

When Israel made the choice for an earthly king, she declared a preference for mediocrity rather than the holiness and separation required by the Lord. Even after attaining and living in the promises like Israel did, we can still lose our focus on God. When we start to put our security in that which we can predict and control rather than keeping it focused on God, we are about to depart from His rule. This is precisely the problem that turns new wineskins into old ones, and it can happen faster than most of us would ever expect.

The Lord was gracious and answered Israel's demands for a king. He even gave them one who appealed to their desires, being "head and shoulders" taller than others. He looked good and appeared powerful. Saul was a king they could understand and relate to. Having a king enabled Israel to camouflage her distinctive calling by making her more like the surrounding nations. This provided security, but in the wrong thing.

Very few people enjoy being "different." Almost every true move of God, even those which have attained extraordinary success and tasted the fruit of God's promises, has ultimately regressed into an organization that is more comparable to a corporation than to the biblical church. Even after we have entered the Promised Land of God, this yoke of conformity remains a powerful and deceptive trap. Without vigilance in keeping our focus on the Lord, we can fall at any time to its power.

In time, King Saul revealed his true nature. The elders of Israel had wanted to do things their own way and Saul emerged as a personification of that self-will. But the people understood and identified with this, so they continued to follow him.

Remarkably, even when Saul became demented the people continued to follow him, reflecting the same demonic loyalty to Saul that many a tortured and abused wife or daughter has demonstrated to a husband or father. In both instances, people are incomprehensibly protective of the very ones who cruelly afflict them. This type of loyalty is not noble; it is sad evidence of a destroyed human soul. This tyranny of the familiar that has been joined to the yoke of conformity, may be one of the most illogical bondages a person can have. It is also one of the strongest.

When the time came to replace Saul, the Lord sent the prophet Samuel to Jesse and his sons. Samuel was a great prophet, but he too was at times afflicted with the yoke of bondage to the familiar. When Samuel arrived at the house of Jesse, he began to reason according to his own expectations. Based on what he was familiar with, he started looking for another man of physical stature like Saul.

However, even though the Lord chose one whose *heart* was that of a prophet and a king, David's outward appearance was that of a shepherd boy. David was a man **"after God's own heart" (I Samuel 13:14).** He was one who sought the favor of God first, not the favor of men. The people could not relate to this, and it took them a long time before they could fully accept David. Likewise, it has almost always taken the people of God a long time to recognize those with true spiritual authority.

As the years passed and Saul's days came to an end, it became clear to Judah that David was the Lord's anointed. Judah appointed David king, but Israel was not as quick to follow. Although the Lord had spoken, their misguided loyalty to the house of Saul caused Israel to keep Saul's offspring on the throne, being determined to stay with the familiar.

Those in Israel continued looking for Saul when they should have been looking at David. This same choice faces the church in every generation. Will we continue our blind and misguided loyalty to the old and familiar order, or will we give our loyalty to a new order that is unfamiliar, but is chosen by God?

One of the greatest men of God in the last century, Andrew Murray, prayed fervently for revival for most of his life. When it came, he rejected it, because it did not come in the form that he was expecting. Today much of the church now expects a coming revival. Pastors admonish their people to pray for revival, but at the same time often resist the ministry of those being raised up to prepare the church for the new move. Fearful of error and fanaticism, the church often frantically seeks for that which God has *already provided*, though we have not been able to recognize it.

If God's "new move" does not come in the way we expect, we have been more prone to reject it than to embrace it, regardless of how much we have preached about the need for a new move. How long will the church go on proclaiming openness to "all that God has," while at the same time restricting His movements to the controllable and predictable, to situations suited to our present experiences and doctrines?

Interestingly, the churches and individuals who often give the most lip service to preaching and predicting that God was going to do a new thing have been the most prone to resist change! Some preach most fervently what they are actually the most afraid of. They seem to think that just preaching it is enough to protect them from the reality.

Reactionary preaching is often a reflection of a preacher's own bondage. The church was rocked when a champion of the national anti-pornography campaign turned out to be bound to pornography himself. Many cult watchers have turned out to hold doctrines and practices worse than the cults they try to keep our attention focused on.

As Paul said, **"For we can do nothing *against* the truth, but only for the truth" (II Corinthians 13:8).** The gospel is not reactionary. It is not against others. The gospel is for the truth. The truth, when revealed, will automatically dispel the darkness. If we would spend more time revealing what is true than worrying about the false, our light would quickly reveal and overpower the false.

Likewise, if we preach "a new thing" in reaction to the old, we are doomed to turn the new wineskin into an old one just as our predecessors did. It is not just a new *thing* that we need. We need a new *heart*—a heart that has its faith and security in God. We don't need a new environment, or even a new wineskin, because even a new wineskin is useless if we do not have new wine to put in it.

If we just get one more "new thing" or new truth or new form of worship, those will also become old wineskins very quickly. New wine does need a new wineskin; but the wine is not for the wineskin—the wineskin is for the new wine. We do not need a new wineskin until we have new wine.

I have not found a single example in church history of new wine ever being produced by those whose attention was given to first finding a new wineskin. This is not to conclude that it cannot happen; but since it has apparently never happened yet, it may well be that God simply refuses to work that way. On the contrary, every new movement that has received new wine has then found a new wineskin to hold it.

The first-century church did not even have a wineskin; they made it up as they went! They made the wineskin to hold the reality of what was happening in their midst. When we seek a new wineskin before having new wine, it is usually reactionary. If we seek new wine, we will be given the wisdom at the proper time to make the appropriate wineskin.

Restoration *and* Renewal

Almost all the great reformers in church history, such as Luther, Wesley and Zinzendorf, tried to stay in their mother churches to see them reformed. Only when it became impossible to remain where they were did they begin a new movement. We must not use this truth concerning the "bondage to the familiar" to consider everything that we are familiar with to be bad.

As Paul told the Corinthians, "**Now I praise you because you remember me in everything, and** *hold firmly to the traditions,* **just as I delivered them to you"** (I Corinthians 11:2). As one friend of mine said, "Traditions are the living faith of dead men. *Traditionalism* is the dead faith of living men."

We will not become a new wineskin just by becoming reactionary to everything that is a tradition. We must put our faith in God and not in our environment, whether it is new or old. God did not say that He was going to make *all new things,* but that He was going to make *all things new.* This speaks of the process of renewal.

Since the Reformation began, there has been a conflict between Renewal and Restoration theology. It is quite apparent that God is doing both. The wise will bring from their treasures things both old and new. Many seemingly rigid and inflexible denominations now have more life and power from God than the "new wineskin" churches which have become reactionary. Many (though not all) "nondenominational" churches have fallen into a terrible spirit of pride, sectarianism and territorial preservation that is just as strong as anything found in the denominational churches.

On the other hand, there are many denominational churches in which there is almost no sectarian spirit. These denominational churches are open to the whole church and more open to the new things that God is doing than many who were on the forefront of the most recent moves of God. **"God is opposed to the proud, but gives grace to the humble" (James 4:6).** He does this regardless of the sign they may have over their door.

God is bringing forth new wineskins *and* He is renewing some of the older wineskins. In biblical times, there was a process for renewing an old and brittle wineskin so that it could be used again. First the wineskin was soaked in hot water. This would expand the molecules. Then it was dipped in hot oil which could be absorbed. This treatment would make the wineskin as flexible as a new one. When the Word of God (the water) becomes "hot" to us again, and not cold or lukewarm, it will expand and prepare us so that when the anointing comes it will soak in and make us flexible again.

As the apostle Paul stated it, **"that He might present to Himself the church in all her glory,** *having no spot or wrinkle* **or any such thing; but that she should be holy and blameless" (Ephesians 5:27).** That the church will be without spot speaks of being cleansed from sin. That she will be without wrinkle speaks of a perpetual youthfulness—she will not age! The bride of Christ will have a heart that keeps her fresh and young. The church will have this nature before her Bridegroom returns for her.

Chapter 12

THE CREATED WILL BE CREATIVE

Our blessed Creator really is that—creative! The diversity of the creation is unfathomable in its glory and genius. He made every snowflake, every tree, and every one of us different. Clearly, He loves diversity. Why then is the church, which should most reflect the nature of God, so boringly uniform? Does this not represent a radical departure from our commission to represent the Lord on this earth?

When the Lord made man in His image, He obviously made us creative. Why then do we allow the church to continue submitting to the mentality that so stifles creativity? Does our glorious God really accept worship that is just learned and repeated by rote, which could just as easily be offered by a parrot, or a computer?

One of the most remarkable stories in the New Testament concerns the two men on the road to Emmaus. The resurrected Jesus attaches Himself to their company. Having listened to their tragic story of His death by crucifixion, Jesus begins to expound the Scriptures concerning Himself. Here we have Christ preaching Christ. It does not get anymore anointed than that! But they still could not recognize Him! Why? Mark 16:12 reveals the answer: **"He appeared in *a different form.*"**

Obviously, the Lord appeared to them in a different form for a reason. We must understand that reason if we are to recognize the Lord when He draws near to us. *If we are going to know the living Christ, we must know Him by the Spirit and not by appearances.*

Spiritual Bigotry

How many times do we fail to recognize the Lord because He comes to us in a form that we are not used to? If we become comfortable with the Pentecostal "form," we will not recognize the Lord if He tries to come to us through a Baptist. If we become used to the charismatic "form," we will not recognize Him if He tries to come to us as a Pentecostal. If we have grown up in the Third Wave Movement, we will have a hard time receiving the Lord if He tries to come to us in any other form than the one we are accustomed to.

The reason for these prejudices is a subtle form of *racism*. Racism is far more than a black-white or Jew-Gentile issue. Racism is one of the most base forms of pride. It is pride in the flesh, or externals. Racism promotes the bondage to the familiar, a bondage which can rob us of our closest encounters with our Lord.

When the Lord lamented over Jerusalem for killing the prophets and those who were sent to her, He declared that her house was being left desolate. She would not see Him again until she said, **"Blessed is He who comes in the name of the Lord" (Matthew 23:39).** What He spoke to Jerusalem, He also spoke to the church, the spiritual Jerusalem. We will not see the Lord until we learn to bless those who come in His name.

From the time of Jesus' resurrection, it has been His practice to come in a different form than the one we are familiar with. In this way, the Lord continues to strike blows at that which will always lead to a desolate house—our spiritual pride in the petty little forms we uphold as the custodians of "the present move of God."

The God who stretched out the heavens like a tent curtain is too big to dwell exclusively in our little denominations, regardless of how big they become. He is too big to be found exclusively in our snappy new form of worship, or the old one. He is much bigger than our ability to perceive. His ways will always exceed the neat little boxes that we try to keep Him in. Therefore it will only be those who can see beyond any mere form who will ever really behold Him to any degree.

Nothing hinders our ability to receive revelation more than pride. It was for this reason that Jesus thanked the

Father, praying, **"Thou didst hide these things from the wise and intelligent and didst** *reveal them to babes"* **(Matthew 11:25).** A baby is small and young and knows that it must grow. A baby knows that it must learn and does not know very much. When we lose the humility of a baby, we lose the ability to receive what the Father is revealing.

Seeking God's Grace

"**God is opposed to the proud, but gives grace to the humble" (James 4:6).** There is nothing that will separate us from God more than our pride, of which racism and many other sins are but symptoms. Possibly no pride is greater than the belief that God is just like us! When we lose the character of the little child who is ever open, seeking and learning, we have departed from the grace of God, which is only given to the humble.

When the Lord returns He will, as promised, separate those who have the nature of goats from those with the nature of sheep. One of the distinguishing tests will be this: **"I was a** *stranger,* **and you invited Me in" (Matthew 25:35).** A foreigner is someone different from us. He is from a different place. He may speak a different language. He may even be from a different denomination.

One of the primary factors God will use to distinguish us as either a sheep or a goat is whether we are open to those who are different from us. Such openness is an irrefutable test of true humility. An openness to the foreigner is required if we are to receive the grace of God.

The Israelites were commanded, **"Show your love for the alien, for you were aliens in the land of Egypt" (Deuteronomy 10:19).** The implication is that one reason the Lord allowed Israel to be held captive in a foreign land was so that they would develop compassion for foreigners.

In addition to the humility that was worked in Israel during her captivity, another important reason for their compassion for the foreigner is stated in Deuteronomy 31:12: **"Assemble the people, the men and the women and children and the *alien [foreigner]* who is in your town, *in order that they may hear and learn and fear the LORD your God,* and be careful to observe all the words of this law."**

The Foundation of Spiritual Authority

True spiritual authority is founded on compassion. It was because Jesus felt compassion for the sheep who were without a shepherd that he became our Shepherd. He felt compassion for those who lived in darkness so He became their Teacher and their Light.

We will only have true spiritual authority to the degree that we have Jesus' compassion. We will have no compassion for those whom we scorn, belittle, or reject because they are different. We will never have true authority to correct the doctrines of another movement or denomination until we have *God's love* for that movement or denomination. Without love we will not have a true ministry. The walls we erect with our prejudices are in conflict with love and in conflict with God Himself.

Regardless of their wrong doctrines or how antiquated a church's form of worship may be, if they love the poor, the orphans, the widows and the foreigners, God will bless and take care of them. *He will do this because they love and care for the ones He wants to care for.* One of the main reasons God has so blessed America is because America's doors have been more open to the foreigner and the oppressed than possibly any other nation in history. We have not always treated our immigrants well after they arrived, but we took them in.

Loving the Foreigner

It is not always necessary to go to a foreign nation to reach that nation with the gospel. Almost every major nation is represented in the student body of many of our universities. At one recent count, sixty of the world leaders had been educated in the United States. Most foreign students are lonely. They are far from family, friends and culture and are wide open to the gospel. In one poll, foreign students said their greatest desire, second only to getting a good education, was to have an American friend.

Unfortunately, many foreign students are spending their time at our universities isolated and ostracized. The man who planned the Japanese attack on Pearl Harbor and the man who commanded the Japanese forces during that attack were both educated in the United States. Both of these men returned home from school offended by the racist treatment they received in America. How might history have been changed if they had been treated differently?

A significant number of Islamic leaders who now call the U.S. "the great Satan" were also educated here. How might our present world be different if we had loved and befriended the students while they were in our country? Our future can be greatly impacted if we will repent of our racism and begin to love the foreigners in our midst. Even more importantly, how will our standing on the judgment day be different if we open our hearts to those who are different from us?

This is not to advocate capturing the foreigners who are among us to force them to listen to our "witness." True love and tolerance for the foreigners will open their hearts. Then they will be open to understanding the reasons for our kindness. A demonstrated love for those who are different from us is a striking contrast to the hate, fear and intolerance that is the natural state of fallen mankind, and the fruit of many of the world's religions. Curiosity and questions are inevitable when we demonstrate love.

Paul stated that **"the kindness of God leads you to repentance" (Romans 2:4).** The word Islam means "submission." Fear can bring someone into submission. Only God's love can free us for a true repentance.

In Deuteronomy 14:28-29 and 26:12 we see that the tithe was for the Levite *and* the alien, the orphan and the widow. With all of our emphasis upon tithing, have we been putting our tithe in the right place? Presently, less than one tenth of one percent of the budget of the Christian church in America is spent on missions. We may be doing more for missions than any other country, but that does not mean that we are doing enough!

This issue of caring for the foreigners is so important that when Paul listed the qualifications for leadership in the church, one of the qualifications was that the prospective overseer had to be given to hospitality for *foreigners* (see I Timothy 3:2 and Titus 1:8). The Greek word that is translated "hospitality" in these texts is *philoxenos*, a word which literally denotes "hospitality to strangers or foreigners."

Clearly the Lord makes an issue of our being open to foreigners. It is His way of dealing with our racism and prejudices which separate us from Him and from one another. Again, this is not just an issue involving the color of our skin. The spirit of racism separates Methodists from Baptists and charismatics from Pentecostals or Presbyterians. Racism is pride in the flesh, or externals.

As Paul declared, **"We are the true circumcision, who worship in the Spirit of God and glory in Christ Jesus *and put no confidence in the flesh"* (Philippians 3:3).**

The Test

One of the most sure signs that we have come to worship in Spirit and Truth and to glory in Christ Jesus is when we are able to look beyond the externals to know one another after the Spirit instead of the flesh. If our confidence is in being a Baptist, or a charismatic, or a nondenominational

Christian, we have not yet understood what it really means to be joined to Christ.

For all of you who were baptized into Christ have clothed yourselves with Christ.

There is neither Jew nor Greek, there is neither slave nor free man, there is neither male nor female; *for you are all one in Christ Jesus"* **(Galatians 3:27-28).**

Racism is also the primary reason why the issue of "natural" Israel will not go away until the church faces it. For about two thousand years, the Lord dealt almost exclusively with the Jews as His covenant people. Now for nearly two thousand years He has dealt primarily with Gentile believers as His covenant people. Now we are coming to the end of the times of the Gentiles. What is emerging is not another "time of the Jews." It is the time of grafting together the **"two into one new man" (Ephesians 2:15).** What is now emerging is the time of the Jews and the Gentiles together *in unity.*

Because **"God is opposed to the proud, but gives grace to the humble" (James 4:6),** He is using this issue to bring both the church and Israel to the place of humility that will enable us to receive His grace. It takes humility and a certain deliverance from our self-centeredness for the church to see God's purpose with the nation of Israel. It will likewise take humility and a deliverance from self-centeredness for Israel to recognize God's purpose in the church. Neither can be seen except through Christ Jesus. **"For He Himself is our peace,** *who made both groups into one, and broke down the barrier of*

the dividing wall, by abolishing in His flesh the enmity"
(Ephesians 2:14-15).

Pride brings God's resistance. Just as pride led to man's first fall, it is the root cause of every fall from grace—which brings death. That is why Paul warned the church, **"Do not become arrogant towards the branches...for if God did not spare the natural branches, neither will He spare you" (Romans 11:18, 21).** One of the true proofs that we are abiding in Christ is that in Him the barrier, or dividing wall is broken down. Our arrogance toward another part of the body cuts us off from God and from His grace. These can only be received through our humility.

The issue of the "natural branches" is meant to challenge the church to humility and obedience, just as the Tree of the Knowledge of Good and Evil was placed in the garden of Eden for the same reason. The Tree of Knowledge was not put in the garden just as a stumbling block. It was at that tree that our first parents were given a place to demonstrate their humility before God and their obedience to Him.

This tree with both "natural" and "spiritual" branches is the same to both the church and Israel—it is a point where we will choose either humility and obedience or, like Adam and Eve, a place where we can indeed be cut off from God's purposes. If we are to abide in Christ, there can be no dividing walls; there must be humility.

The issue is not just Jew/Gentile—it is humility and obedience. The church is the point where Israel is confronted with humility and obedience or arrogance and disobedience. Israel is the point where the church is confronted with the same issues. When both Israel and the church have overcome this barrier to being grafted together, through Christ, both will have attained to such a place of humility and obedience that an unprecedented measure of God's grace and power can be released.

When we have attained to this humility which can release such grace and power, it will be enough to overcome every other enemy—including death! That is why the apostle could so confidently declare that when the Jews are grafted back into the tree, **"what will their acceptance be but *life from the dead?"* (Romans 11:15)** They will receive resurrection power—the conquering of the last enemy.

The Evil of Pseudo Tolerance

Usually we who believe that we are free of the spirit of racism will only have tolerance and acceptance if the "race" in question becomes like us. The Baptists will gladly accept the Presbyterians, just as soon as they immerse their people! The Pentecostals will gladly accept the Methodists, just as soon as they speak in tongues. The list goes on.

The white church loves the blacks and wants more of them in *their* church, but there are very few whites who want to join a black church. Most of what we believe to be a tearing down of the dividing walls is still rooted in the arrogance of having *our* own terms met and making everyone else like us.

The church loves to see the Jews converted—as long as they become a part of the church. This "Messianic Movement," however, is an affront. Neither the church nor the Messianic movement are a true reflection of the new creation. I will not come into unity with my wife by making her a man! Our unity will come when we see how our differences compliment one another, rather than how they bring conflict.

Paul explained, **"That in Himself He might make the two into one new man, thus establishing peace, and might reconcile them *both* in one body to God through the cross, by it having put to death the enmity" (Ephesians 2:15-16).**

When the enmity is put to death between the black and white races the black men are not going to turn white! For there to be unity of purpose and peace between them, the Jews are not required to become Gentiles any more than the Gentiles are required to become citizens of Israel.

Just as a body needs many different parts to live (a heart, lungs, liver, etc.), Christ's body needs its many *different* parts. These parts are supposed to remain different, but *function together*. The Lutherans, Baptists, Pentecostals, charismatics and others have each added truths to the church which are needed for us to accomplish our end time mandate. With all our progress during the Reformation, the church's foundation is still more in Rome than in Jerusalem or Antioch.

As Paul stated, **"It is not you [the Gentiles] who supports the root, but the root [the Jews] supports you" (Romans**

11:18). When Israel is grafted back in, she will help the church return to her true roots, something she has not yet been able to do. This is not to be misunderstood, thinking that we are to return to the Law or to Mosaic rituals. The reason for our unity is far more profound than that. Even the Messianic Movement, as a whole, has not yet comprehended this.

The issue is our deliverance from the fears which keep us bound to the tyranny of the familiar. Without deliverance from this fear, we will remain unable to receive change. We will also continue to be unable to receive our awesome God, because He will not come in the petty little forms that we have contrived to contain Him.

We must be delivered from the pride that causes us to presume that God is just like we are. The Lord has made the focal point of this issue the dividing wall between the natural and spiritual seeds of Abraham, because the basic conflict is between that which is flesh and that which is spirit. However, all other dividing walls must come down as well.

Until we overcome our racism, our bondage to the familiar, and the tendency to place our security in our environment, we will continue on the road to Emmaus. We will remain so caught up in our own little worlds that even if the Lord Himself draws near to us, we will not recognize Him.

Chapter 13

UNITY
AND
POWER

Even though Israel was a single nation, it was composed of different tribes, each with different callings and functions in the overall plan of God. One important lesson Israel had to learn in the wilderness was how the different tribes were to march together and function in unity.

The same is true of the body of Christ; the church is *meant* to be made up of different "streams" or "spiritual tribes," but we will not enter the Promised Land until we have learned to march and function together as a single spiritual nation. There are supposed to be differences in the body of Christ, but the differences are supposed to compliment each other, not conflict.

Jesus Is Returning for a Bride— Not a Harem!

The apostle Paul made a radical statement. If we believed it and acted on it, we would create the greatest reformation in church history. He simply stated, "**There is *one* body and one Spirit, just as also you were called in one hope of your calling**" (Ephesians 4:4).

In the Lord's eyes there is only *one* church or body of believers. When we begin to see by the Spirit, we will see only one church. Every true believer in Jesus is a member of the same eternal family with the same Father. This is not an idealistic hope—it is a present reality. This is not to be blind to the endless sects, divisions and denominations presently within the church, but we are to give a higher regard to the biblical testimony of God. The church will come into a true unity.

Though there are supposed to be different callings and streams of emphasis within the church, the Lord has never recognized or endorsed the many divisions created by men. God never changes—if we are going to be of one mind with Him, we are the ones who will have to change. This change regarding our understanding and recognition of the church will soon sweep the world as fast as the changes which took place in Eastern Europe during the late 1980s.

The political changes that have taken and are taking place in the natural realm of human politics merely reflect the activity in the spiritual realm. The walls that separate people are coming down. If the leaders do not take them down, the people will. The leaders of Eastern Europe who tried to resist the change were themselves swept away by it. The same will be true of the leaders of the church who do not recognize the signs of the times and try to resist that which is irresistible.

The only identity given to the biblical church was a geographical identity. Each church was named after the city in which it was located. There was the church at Corinth, the church at Rome, the church at Jerusalem, the church at Ephesus, the church at Smyrna, etc. Never did the Lord recognize a church according to any characteristic other than its location.

If we are going to be a biblical people, we have no choice but to do the same. By giving recognition to the mere human identities, we have allowed and even promoted the divisions in the church. That day is coming to an end. Jesus is not returning for a harem. He is returning for a bride—singular.

In the one church, there are supposed to be differences but not divisions. The church contains a unity of diversity, not a unity of conformity. If the church is to function properly, there must be different types of congregations. The Lord and the apostles often used certain metaphors to describe spiritual realities. The church was often referred to as the Lord's body because it has the characteristics of a physical body. In a physical body, the most healthy heart will still die without healthy lungs, kidneys and other vital organs. The same is true of the church.

The different organs of the body do not compete with one another unless there is cancer in the body. Cancer is basically made up of cells that determine that they are going to grow without regard to the rest of the body. Self-centered congregations that promote their own growth without regard to the rest of the church in their region could likewise be called cancers in the body of Christ.

We are all members of one another, and we need each other if the body is to be healthy. Just as a liver that begins to grow without regard to the heart, lungs and other organs is allowing its selfishness to ultimately put its own existence in jeopardy, congregations that esteem their own growth above the needs of the whole body are ultimately condemning themselves.

Each congregation must have its own vision, but it must be a vision which fits with the rest of what the Lord is doing in His church. The most healthy heart will die without proper interchange with the other organs. The most healthy congregation will ultimately lose its life if it does not have interchange with the rest of the body, especially those congregations that are different from itself. To be spiritually alive, the church is absolutely dependent upon the proper interchange between the different "organs" of its makeup.

Geographical Unity

The Lord and the apostles recognized the church only by its geographical location for a good reason: Those who are committed in obedience to His Word are to find their identity in relation to the other local expressions of His body. Long-distance relationships with those who relate to the same truths or emphases require little growth or maturity to maintain. An arm located several miles from the rest of my body would be of little use to me. Likewise, we are of little use to the Lord's body if we are not fitly joined to those with whom we daily function in a real and living relationship.

The church in each locality must learn to properly interrelate and function together if there is to be life in the body. As the conflict consummates at the end of this age, it will be as true of the church as it was of the original thirteen American colonies who were told that they must "join or die."

Even a cursory look at the present condition of the church reveals glaring inadequacies. In some places, there are three congregations located on the same block who have little or no interchange. They duplicate the same ministries and functions and, more than likely, are each trying to sustain buildings that are only one third full.

How much more of our resources could be released and devoted to the true work and gospel commission if only the obvious duplications were eliminated? With our present lack of intercommunication and relationship, a false prophet or teacher can enter a congregation, wreck it, and after being discovered, just walk across the street and do the same thing all over again. Paul told the Ephesians that this would *not* happen when the body was properly joined together:

> As a result, we are no longer to be children, tossed here and there by waves, and carried about by every wind of doctrine, by the trickery of men, by craftiness in deceitful scheming;
>
> but speaking the truth in love, we are to grow up in all aspects into Him, who is the head, even Christ,
>
> from whom the whole body, being fitted and held together by that which every joint supplies,
>
> according to the proper working of each individual part, causes the growth of the body for the building up of itself in love (Ephesians 4:14-16).

The church consistently gets tossed about by every new wind of doctrine, trickery, craftiness and deceit because we have not yet been properly joined.

Nothing is impossible with God. He could have us all believing the same about every doctrine if He so desired, but that would not result in a true joining. The Lord is more concerned with having us love each other than with having us in perfect doctrinal agreement. Doctrines are not a basis for unity; they are a basis for division.

True spiritual unity is based on unity of function, purpose and love for one another, and not just on agreement about every doctrine. The tribes of Israel were commanded to be in unity in only two basic areas: worship and warfare. They were to worship Jehovah only in the place where He chose to dwell, and if one of the tribes was attacked, they were all to respond as a single nation. In all other areas there could be diversity.

Much of the disunity in the church is the result of our trying to unify areas that the Lord has not given us the grace to unify.

Being in unity does not require us to drop all denominational or movement affiliations. We are not required to come under one giant organization or to drop all organizational affiliation. The time may come when denominational organizations are no longer needed, but presently they are serving the purpose of keeping congregations focused on the vision they need to have without them feeling compelled to be just like the other parts of the body in their area.

We must have diversity if the church is going to focus like a body. Until we cast off all the insecurities that require an unrighteous conformity, the different denominations and movements are probably necessary. As Paul explained, there are varieties of ministries and gifts. The body is made up of many members, not just one, and the foot cannot say to the hand that because it is not a foot it is not a part of the body (see I Corinthians 12:4-15). We must recognize the differences which are ordained by God and see in them how we may function together, not apart.

How the World Will Believe

In the New Testament, churches were named after the city of their residence because *God loves the cities*. When Jesus came to Jerusalem He did not weep over the temple; He wept over the city. When we think of cities, we usually think of buildings, shopping centers and businesses. Jesus does not see cities that way; He sees people. The church is given to the cities to be the light of those cities and to win the people who reside there.

When Jesus prayed for His church He prayed that she would be **"perfected in unity, that the world may know that Thou didst send Me" (John 17:23).** The world will not believe the gospel until it sees the church in unity. The increasing unity of the church will be the greatest evangelistic power ever released. The church will not come into its perfection or maturity until it comes into unity.

True unity will not come through compromise or political agreements between the leaders of different camps. In the Lord's prayer for the unity of His people, He declared how it would come: **"The *glory* which Thou hast given Me I have given to them; that they may be one, just as We are one" (John 17:22).** We are changed by seeing the glory of the Lord (II Corinthians 3:18). When the Lamb enters, all the elders will cast their crowns at His feet (Revelation 4:10).

Who can presume glory or position in His presence? When we turn our attention upon Him, jealousy and selfish ambition will be replaced with a consuming passion to see Jesus glorified and receive the reward of His sacrifice.

Psalm 133 has been titled "The Psalm of Unity." It is a simple and plain statement of how the church will come into unity:

> **Behold, how good and how pleasant it is for brothers to dwell together in unity!**

> It is like the precious oil upon the *head*, coming down upon the beard, even Aaron's beard, coming down upon the edge of his robes.
>
> It is like the dew of Hermon, coming down upon the mountains of Zion; for *there* the LORD commanded the blessing—life forever (Psalm 133).

Aaron was a biblical type of Christ, the High Priest of God. As we anoint Jesus, the Head, with our worship and devotion, we will see the oil flow down until it covers the rest of the body, bringing us into that good and pleasant unity.

The church will never become what it was called to be until she gets her attention off of herself and back onto the Lord. We have all been worshipers of the temple of the Lord instead of the Lord of the temple. What good is the most glorious temple if the Lord is not in it? If He is in it, it will not be the temple that gets our attention! It is the glory that causes change. It is the glory that brings unity. It is the glory of the Lord for which the temple was made, and His glory will fill that temple.

The Ministry

John the Baptist, the harbinger of the New Covenant Age, is possibly the most perfect model for New Covenant ministry. His whole purpose was to point to the Lamb of God and prepare the way for Him. He was then willing to decrease as He increased. That is the true purpose of all ministry—to point to Jesus, prepare the way for Him, and then be willing to decrease in our own authority with people as their relationship to Him grows.

When John the Baptist pointed out Jesus to John and Andrew, they began to follow Him. Jesus then turned and asked them a question, the most important question of their lives: **"What do you seek?" (John 1:38)** What is it that we are seeking as we follow Him? Is it healing? Prosperity? Recognition? Eternal life? Are we just seeking peace of mind? These first two followers of Jesus answered His question with a most appropriate question in return: **"Rabbi...where dwellest thou?" (verse 38 KJV)**

Where is that place where the Lord can dwell? There are many places that the Lord will bless. There are a few more that He will visit, but *where is that place where the Lord can dwell?* The Son of Man is still seeking a place to lay His head—a place where He can be the head. Much of what we are calling His churches are in fact no more than franchises. We have mostly been building temples for the people rather than for the Lord. Where is His temple? Where is *His* dwelling place?

Woodrow Wilson once said that many people were defeated by secondary successes. Good can be the worst enemy of best. We cannot understand the complete purpose of any single aspect of the church until we understand that whole purpose of the church. We cannot be satisfied by our individual accomplishments, but only with the fulfillment of the entire church's purpose. The High priest carried the stones of all the tribes of Israel on his heart. If we are going to walk in the high calling of God, we must have all of God's people on our heart.

We must keep our vision focused upon the ultimate purpose of God or we will be distracted by the lessor purposes of God. The ultimate purpose of God is that all things be summed up in His Son. Even the church coming into her maturity and glory is but a means to this end. The church is given for the purpose of lifting up the Son and being the place where He can dwell.

I have had a recurring vision of a pastor. When this pastor focuses his attention on the Lord, great multitudes gather around him. Every time he takes his attention off of the Lord to look at the people, they begin to scatter from him. The people are coming for the Lord, not us. If they are coming for us, then they have been deceived and misled. Our personalities or abilities may be able to draw a crowd, but only the Lord can draw them for the right reasons and make them into His dwelling place.

Our quest is to work with the Lord to build the church that He wants to live in, not just one that will draw people. When a church is built that the Lord can dwell in, we will have far more people than we know what to do with. When He is truly lifted up He will draw all men to Himself. The true church will be built on those who are drawn to Him, not just to a good preacher, a certain style of worship, or to a doctrine, but to Him.

Chapter 14

CROSSING
OVER

There is a reason why we have been called out of Egypt. It is to learn all that we must in the wilderness, so that we can conquer the Promised Land. We usually relate to the promises of God on a personal basis, and that is valid, but there is much more. As we mature, we become more concerned with the Lord receiving *His* inheritance in and through the church than with what we may personally attain.

The heathen are the Lord's inheritance, and the ends of the earth are His possession (Psalm 2:8). More wonderful than attaining our own personal wealth is seeing the salvation of the lost. It was no accident that Israel crossed over into the Promised Land during the harvest season (Joshua 3:15).

When the church starts to enter her inheritance, it will be the beginning of the greatest harvest the world has ever seen.

In Joshua we can see an outline of how we, too, will enter into our inheritance and possess the promises of God. The Jordan River is often representative of death in Scripture because it empties into the Dead Sea. That is why both John the Baptist and Jesus baptized there.

Paul said, **"Now these things happened to them as an example, and they were written for our instruction, upon whom the ends of the ages have come" (I Corinthians 10:11).** Scripture relates that Israel was crossing the Jordan into her inheritance at a very hazardous time: **"The Jordan overflows all its banks all the days of harvest" (Joshua 3:15).** This is a testimony that death would be overflowing during the very time of the harvest and our crossing over into our inheritance. This corroborates the Lord's testimony that the end of the age is the harvest, but it is also the greatest time of trouble the world has ever known (Matthew 13:39, 24:1-44).

Despite the persecutions and troubles, we can be encouraged. As soon as the priests who were carrying the Ark stepped into the Jordan, the waters (of death) were rolled back **"a great distance away at *ADAM!*" (Joshua 3:16)** When we finally get in line to follow the Ark of God, which is Jesus, who entered this Jordan 2,000 cubits (years) ahead of us (verse 4), there will be victory over every consequence of sin which has come down all the way from Adam. As the Lord spoke through Isaiah:

Arise, shine; for your light has come, and the glory
of the LORD has risen upon you.

For behold, darkness will cover the earth, and deep
darkness the peoples; but the LORD will rise upon you,
and His glory will appear upon you.

And nations will come to your light, and kings to the
brightness of your rising.

Lift up your eyes round about, and see; they all
gather together, they come to you. Your sons will
come from afar, and your daughters will be carried
in the arms.

Then you will see and be radiant, and your heart will
thrill and rejoice; because the abundance of the sea will
be turned to you, the wealth of the nations will come to
you (Isaiah 60:1-5).

During the worst of times, when darkness is covering the
earth and deep darkness the people, the glory of the Lord is
going to rise upon His people. Then the people will gather
to the church in the greatest harvest the world has ever seen.

Humility Before Exaltation

After Israel crossed the Jordan, they were allowed to
proceed no further until the young men who had been born
in the wilderness had been circumcised. Circumcision speaks
of the removal of the flesh, or the carnal nature. The
circumcisions were performed in Gilgal just outside the walls
of Jericho. By these circumcisions Israel was humiliated and
made weak right before their enemies.

Consider the parallel of this to what has been happening to the church for the past few years! It has been difficult to endure the humiliation, but all that has happened is part of God's plan. Before we can conquer the strongholds which are now possessing our land, a humiliation is required. **"Humble yourselves, therefore, under the mighty hand of God, that He may exalt you at the proper time" (I Peter 5:6).**

For their own sakes, the Lord has consistently humbled His people before He has exalted them. He made Joseph a slave, and then sent him to the dungeon before making him one of the most powerful men of his time. The Israelites were enslaved in Egypt for centuries before God could make her the place of His habitation, and reveal His power through her. Moses, after dwelling in the palaces of Egypt, had to shepherd sheep for forty years, the most humble profession of the times. David had to live in caves and spend years fleeing from the very people he was called to rule before he could take his place at their head.

We must learn to see humiliation as one of our greatest opportunities to be promoted by God. The more humiliation that we will endure, the greater the authority that He can entrust to us.

The humiliation experienced by the body of Christ in recent years has been a circumcision. God has been humbling us and making us weak before our enemies just before we take possession of the very place they are now inhabiting. Let us learn our lessons well during this time. Great power and authority are coming. But if we receive this authority in pride it will only lead to our own fall. Embrace humility and you will one day sit in exaltation.

A Second Passover

After the circumcision, the Israelites celebrated their first Passover in the Promised Land. As we know, *Christ is our Passover* (I Corinthians 5:7). It was the Passover sacrifice that delivered them from their slavery in Egypt—and it is the Passover sacrifice of Christ that delivers us from the Egypt within. The Israelites also partook of the Passover when they entered their Promised Land.

In the same way, it is the Passover sacrifice of Christ that enables us to both escape the present evil age and enter the promises of God. It is the cross that leads us out and the cross that leads us in. The cross is found at the beginning of our journey, and the cross will be found at the end. It is the cross of Jesus that accomplishes everything for His people. If we have truly come to this time, we will begin to see a new emphasis on the cross and what it means for Jesus to be our Passover.

After the circumcision and celebration of the Passover, Israel was ready to go after the walled cities, which represent the enemy's strongholds that we must conquer to possess our Promised Land. We have been given divinely powerful weapons for the destruction of the enemy's strongholds. This is where we begin to use them.

Randall Worley, a pastor in Charlotte, North Carolina, made an insightful statement about the strongholds around our cities. He said, "We cross the physical walls, or boundaries, very easily, passing in and out without hindrance. But we seldom penetrate the spiritual walls of the city. These are the strongholds of pride, prejudice, resentment, rebellion, licentiousness and other spiritual forces. Just as Israel encompassed Jericho, the Lord is now calling His people to encompass and bring down the enemy's strongholds around our cities."

Bringing the Walls Down

These spiritual strongholds will usually be brought down by using the same strategy Joshua used. First, he encompassed the city with the mighty men of war (Joshua 6:3). God's "mighty men of war" are those who have authority with Him because they are mighty in prayer. Many of these "mighty men of war" are actually women.

Those who have the most authority in heaven are usually the inconspicuous men and women who are faithful in prayer. These can accomplish far more for the kingdom than the more conspicuous and eloquent preachers who may have our attention. What is accomplished in the pulpit is usually accomplished more by the prayer behind the pulpit than by the one in it.

If we are to impact our cities with the gospel that sets men free from the enemy's strongholds, we must first encompass our cities with those who are mighty before God. Intercession has, and always will be, one of the most fruitful endeavors of the church. The Lord said that His church would be **"a house of prayer for all the nations" (Mark 11:17).** It is good that we learn to pray for ourselves, but we must mature to the place where we are not only praying for ourselves, but for all the people—for our cities, our schools, our governments, and then other cities, schools, governments, etc.

After Jericho had been encompassed by the mighty men, Joshua then encompassed it with the priests (see verse 4 KJV). Intercession will result in a unity of leadership, and church leaders will then begin to encompass our cities together. The priests carried their own trumpets and rams' horns, which represented their messages. Those messages would come from a great company instead of just individuals.

The priests also carried the Ark, which represented the glory and presence of God. If the Lord is not going up with us, then following even the most biblically precise strategy will accomplish nothing. We are not called to follow formulas and principles—we are called to follow the Lord.

After the priests had marched around Jericho, all the people from every tribe joined in the procession (verse 7). Intercession that encompasses the city will result in a leadership that encompasses the city. These two things will ultimately result in a unified shout of proclamation as the people follow behind their intercessors and leaders. This unified shout of proclamation, given by all the people, will bring the spiritual walls down.

When the Lord looked at what the men of Babel had built, He made an important statement: **"Behold, they are one people, and they all have the same language. And this is what they began to do, and now** *nothing which they purpose to do will be impossible for them"* **(Genesis 11:6).**

Unity is a powerful spiritual force. Jesus told His disciples, **"Again I say to you, that if two of you** *agree* **on earth about anything that they may ask, it shall be done for them by My Father who is in heaven"** (Matthew 18:19). Now the word translated "agree" here implies much more than just an intellectual agreement, but reflects a harmony of nature. This implies that the greater the unity of nature that we come into, the greater the authority that we can have with the Father.

The Father has obligated Himself to answer our prayers when we come into that unity because He knows that we can only attain this by abiding in His Son. Since men's languages were scattered at Babel, the only way a true unity of purpose can ever be achieved again is through the Word, who is God's message to men.

Spiritual authority is multiplied by unity. If the intercessors come into unity, it will result in the spiritual leaders coming into unity. Then the people will follow, and there will be no evil fortress that can stand before us.

He Still Weeps Over the Cities

As stated, when Jesus came to Jerusalem He did not weep over the temple; He wept over the city. When Ezekiel was carried in a vision to Jerusalem, he was told to mark for deliverance those who wept over the abominations of their city. This seems to be a day in which the Lord is again marking those who weep over their cities and is giving them spiritual authority over them.

There are many current testimonies about how prayer has begun to impact spiritual strongholds over cities. There is a city in Iowa where every doctor in town has refused to perform abortions. This was accomplished without passing a single law. There is a city in California where a little group of leaders prayed for the Lord to stop the prostitution business. A few days later the headlines of the local paper noted that, "for unknown reasons," the prostitutes were leaving town.

One day Francis Frangipane and I felt led to pray with a group of leaders from the Washington, D.C. area. We asked the Lord to break the stronghold of deception over Washington. That night, the mayor of Washington was caught in a drug bust. The next day the papers said that narcotics agents had been trying to arrest the mayor for years, but he had "cloaked himself in deception."

We do not presume that a principality was brought down in any of these cases, but the unified prayer by the spiritual leaders in these cities had an immediate impact. A cloak of deception was stripped away, at least briefly, over Washington. However, that is far from the ultimate goal that we should have for that city. If the churches in that area continue to grow in unity and continue their prayers, we will one day see a passionate love for the truth prevail there.

We must not be presumptuous. Very few evil principalities, if any, have yet been brought down. Some have been impacted, however, and many church leaders are beginning to understand the great spiritual authority of a unified church. These are only the small beginnings of a militant church, as we start to go after the gates of hell—the doorways that hell uses to gain access points into our cities, churches, families and every aspect of life.

The battle for Jericho started as the mighty men of war encompassed the city, representing prayer. Then the spiritual leaders and people followed. However, when the walls came down they all had to fight. We cannot cast down principalities with prayer alone. Though we can *cast out* demons, we must *wrestle* with principalities. There must be an actual engaging of the enemy with our sword, the Word of God. But just as the Lord promised Israel: **"Five of you will chase a hundred, and a hundred of you will chase ten thousand"** (**Leviticus 26:8**). With unity there is a multiplication of our spiritual authority.

When the Israelites entered their Promised Land, none of the tribes were allowed to retire from the army until *all* the tribes had possessed their land. The same is true of the church. We are not to stop fighting until all our brothers have gained their inheritance, regardless of their tribe or affiliation. Concerning the church, the adage is certainly true: "one for all and all for one."

Chapter 15

MANNA FROM HEAVEN AND THE SABBATH REST

Let us pause to review our journey with Israel thus far. After going through their Red Sea "baptism," the Israelites were immediately confronted with other major tests. First, the people had to go three days without water. When they finally came to a well, the water was bitter. As with Israel, our first test after our baptism will usually involve learning to turn our bitter water into sweet water. When we are in dry places, we become increasingly desperate for the pure water of God's Word.

When it seems we can go no longer, the word does come, but often it is a bitter or a hard word. This can seem like more than we are able to bear. After great trials we want pure, refreshing encouragement, but that is not always what we need. Whatever God gives to us is what we need. The greater the trials that we can endure, the sooner we can be on our way to the Promised Land.

In modern Western society, where comfort, convenience, security and peace are now demanded as rights, understanding that God plans difficulties for our benefit is incomprehensible to many. God's well-documented ways challenge many modern theologies developed to appease our dread of difficulties. While men are crying **"peace and safety" (I Thessalonians 5:3),** the most difficult times the world has ever known will be sweeping the earth.

Those whose theology assures them that they will be snatched out before tribulation need to realize that the difficulties the Lord said were coming at the end of the age were just **"the *beginning* of birth pangs" (Matthew 24:8).** Even if we are taken out before the great "time of trouble," just enduring the *beginning* of the birth pangs is going to be far beyond the theological grid of this strange new breed of Christians who do not think anything bad should happen to them. In general, the present Western church may be the least prepared of all the people of the earth for the times that are soon coming upon us.

Peter explained that *judgment begins with the household of God* (I Peter 4:17). The word that is translated "judgment" in this passage is the Greek word *krisis* from which we derive our English word *crisis*. One of the definitions given by Webster's for crisis is "the point in a disease in which it is determined if the patient is going to live or die." All of the Old and New Testament prophecies about the end of the age testify that the end will be the greatest time of trouble since the world began. This time of trouble is to begin with the church!

These troubles are not coming as punishment. They are meant to prepare us to not only endure the times, but to shine as lights in the midst of the great darkness. The church is called to be the light of the world. A light is not needed until it is dark. The light is going to shine even more brightly in the great darkness that is coming. As we read previously from Isaiah, **"For behold, darkness will cover the earth, and deep darkness the peoples; but the LORD will rise upon you, and His glory will appear upon you"** (Isaiah 60:2).

At the very time when darkness is covering the earth and deep darkness the peoples, the Lord's glory is rising and appearing upon His church. The judgment, or crisis, that begins with the church is meant to so establish our lives on the kingdom that we cannot be shaken. Then when the whole world begins to shake, we will stand strong and unmoved like a beacon in the fog or a light on a hill. The church is called to lead the way through the impending darkness.

There is a purpose in problems! The Lord did not call us just so we could be comfortable and prosperous here, and then get eternal life as a bonus. We are called to be so strong in faith and moral integrity that we can push back the darkness of our times, regardless of whether we live in the great tribulation or not. Through our wilderness experiences, our faith in God is so established and strengthened that, though the whole world falls apart, we will not be moved, because the world is not our source. Again, if we want to get through the wilderness and start inheriting the promises, we must not waste our trials!

The Lord patiently responded to Israel's complaints about the bitter water, and He gave them a tree to sweeten the water. He then led them to twelve springs of water and let them rest. Perhaps some began to think at this point that they knew how to get their way with God: If they just complained to Him enough, they could get whatever they wanted. Not so!

The Lord is very patient with us. He will often give us what we ask for, even if we don't ask in the right attitude. But that does not mean we have passed the test. As Francis Frangipane observed, "We never really fail God's tests; we just keep taking them until we pass!"

Whether it should be called a failure or simply noted that they did not pass, Israel had to repeat the test. So will we, whenever we respond to our trials with complaining. It would have been understandable for Israel to ask God for water—but to grumble, even in the most trying circumstances, is not the path to the Promised Land. At best, grumbling and complaining leads to a detour which will only make the way longer.

After the people drank the sweet water, they noticed they were hungry, too. Complaining seemed to work the last time, so they tried it again. Of course, they did not grumble directly to the Lord-- they complained to Moses and Aaron. The Lord was not fooled by this, and He is not fooled by us when we try the same thing. Moses responded to them: **"For the LORD hears your grumblings which you grumble against Him. And what are we? Your grumblings are not against us but against the LORD" (Exodus 16:8).**

Regardless of what our problems are, the Lord is the Lord of all. Nothing can happen to us that He does not allow. The enemy cannot get a single blow in while God is not looking. *All complaining is really directed at the Lord, regardless of whom or what we may target.* All complaining is rebellion against Him and the work He is trying to accomplish in us.

Complaining may result in a reprieve from the trial, but it does not result in victory. The Lord gave the people manna and meat as they requested, but they were proceeding down the path that led to their perishing without ever setting foot in the Promised Land. Every trial in the wilderness was actually an opportunity to grow in faith.

The Purpose of Trials

Every test that we endure is for one purpose—promotion. When we pass a trial by believing God, patiently waiting for His provision, we are qualifying for more spiritual authority, which, by the way, also qualifies us for greater trials.

God's miraculous provision is not always a verification that we are on the right path or that our faith achieved the miracle. True faith may even result in a delay of His provision. The testing and purifying of that faith is more precious than the immediate gratification we may be seeking. As the Scriptures testify, the testing of the faithful may be even more intense than the testing of the faithless. The reason for this is because God seeks to raise the faithful to higher and higher standards of victory and spiritual maturity.

The great multitude that is "moving in the Lord" is often just moving in circles. Though they claim to be on their way to the Promised Land, they may actually be just going around and around in the same desert. Some will discern what is happening to them after a few trips around. Many never realize this, and may even think they're in the Promised Land because of all the manna and miracle waters they're receiving.

The signs confirming the right course are clear to the spiritually mature, but to the immature the same signs often appear as dangerous departures from the course because there are so few footprints along the way to confirm that people have traveled this road before. The Lord Jesus warned:

> **Enter by the narrow gate; for the gate is wide, and the way is broad that leads to destruction, and many are those who enter by it.**
>
> **For the gate is small, and the way is narrow that leads to life, and few are those who find it (Matthew 7:13-14).**

The Manna

Jesus also explained that the manna Israel received was a type of Himself:

> **I am the bread of life.**
>
> **Your fathers ate the manna in the wilderness, and they died.**
>
> **This is the bread which comes down out of heaven, so that one may eat of it and not die.**
>
> **I am the living bread that came down out of heaven; if anyone eats of this bread, he shall live forever; and the bread also which I shall give for the life of the world is My flesh (John 6:48-51).**

Jesus is the only satisfaction for the true hunger of the heart. He is the Tree of Life that we were meant to feed on from the beginning. The wilderness is a most difficult place, but it is there that we learn to partake of Jesus every day.

Every morning God provided fresh manna for Israel. It had to be gathered each day and could not be stored for more than one day, except on the day before the Sabbath when none would be provided. If anyone tried to gather more than one day's provision it would become foul. Those who gathered a lot would not have too much and those who gathered little had enough.

Jesus is the Bread from heaven, and this is a testimony to us that we must partake of Him afresh every day. It is useless to try and gather enough of Him to last for the days when we don't want to seek Him. Such bread will only become stale.

What is true about gathering Bread from heaven is equally true concerning the bread we share as ministers of the Word. When we are partaking of fresh manna from heaven we will have fresh manna to give those whom we serve.

This does not necessarily mean that we must have a different word or message every time we preach. Some messages must be preached many times before they become pure. The psalmist declared, **"The words of the LORD are pure words; as silver tried in a furnace on the earth, refined seven times" (Psalm 12:6).** Some words become more pure and penetrating each time they are preached, but we must still go to the Lord and gather that word fresh each time. Otherwise, it will be stale and incapable of imparting life.

The freshness of our message is in the anointing that we receive from the presence of the Lord. There will only be a freshness in our message if we maintain a freshness in our walk with the Lord. How do we maintain this freshness? One of the key factors we need is found in the next lesson Israel was given in the wilderness.

The Sabbath Rest

After the Lord provided manna for Israel, He gave them their first instruction on keeping the Sabbath (see Exodus 16:22-29). This was no accident. Learning to enter the rest of the Lord is a key to receiving fresh manna from heaven.

God had rested on the seventh day of creation. He instituted that His people would likewise rest on the last day of each week. Through more than four thousand years of history, the keeping of the Sabbath continues to be the linchpin of Jewish religion and culture. This certainly signifies its importance. As the Lord said to Israel, **"You shall surely observe My sabbaths; for this is a sign between Me and you throughout your generations, that you may know that I am the LORD who sanctifies you"** (Exodus 31:13).

After the Lord had finished the creation, Genesis records, **"Then God blessed the seventh day and sanctified it, because in it He rested from all His work"** (Genesis 2:3). The only thing different about the seventh day is that God rested on that day. It is not the day that is holy; it is God's rest that is holy. If God had chosen to rest on any other day, then that day would have been holy. God is the one who sanctifies, not the day.

We rest when we abide in the Lord, not just when we observe a certain Sabbath day. God did not rest because He became tired. Isaiah declares, **"The Creator of the ends of the earth does not become weary or tired"** (Isaiah 40:28). God gave the Sabbath rest; the Sabbath did not give God rest. Rest is in God, not in a day.

Baptism is a ritual which symbolizes our commitment to lay down our own lives and interests in order to live for God. Likewise, the Sabbath day is symbolic of something more profound than just not working on one day of the week. The writer of Hebrews equated entering God's rest with entering our Promised Land (see Hebrews 3 and 4). He explained,

"For the one who has entered His rest has himself also rested from his works, as God did from His" (Hebrews 4:10).

Man was created at the end of the sixth day. Adam was God's last work before He rested. Adam's first day was actually God's seventh day of creation. Therefore for Adam to enter into fellowship with God, he had to enter God's rest. This is the focal point of the Sabbath. The Sabbath is not just meant for rest. We are to enter into fellowship with God and into the rest and refreshment that His fellowship provides.

By the time Adam was created, God had already finished the job of creation. There was nothing left for Adam to do but to enjoy the creation and to enjoy the Lord. To fully understand the purpose of the Promised Land for Israel, we must understand God's ultimate purpose to restore man to the place from which he fell. This place was paradise, where God ruled and walked in intimate fellowship with man and the rest of His creation.

The Promised Land of Israel is a prophetic type of the restoration of the earth that will occur during the reign of Christ. But in the meantime, there is a war to be fought in order for us to possess the land. Much of the current theology of prosperity and peace is biblically accurate, but it is out of timing. Some of this theology promotes trying to live in the Promised Land before we have crossed the Jordan, much less removed the giants.

The Lord is using the wilderness experiences to prepare us for the war that is necessary to possess our promises and the peace that will follow. Both the wilderness and the war require faith, spiritual strength, moral purity, and intimacy with the Lord.

Where Rest Is Found

The Lord told Moses, **"My presence shall go with you, and I will give you *rest"* (Exodus 33:14).** A definitive sign that God is truly with us in our ministry is that we have rest. When we are yoked with God, we find rest for our souls; when we are not yoked with Him, we strive and worry.

To be yoked signifies being ready to do heavy work. But when we are yoked with God, it is His energy that accomplishes the task. The apostle Paul claimed to labor more than any of the other apostles, and certainly all them were zealous for the work of the ministry. Those who abide in the Lord will labor, but it will not be toil. It will be a labor of love that brings refreshing and rejuvenation to our souls.

Paul said, **"Whatever you do, do your work heartily, as for the Lord rather than for men" (Colossians 3:23).** When I first worked as a carpenter's helper it was drudgery. Then I determined that I was going to do everything that I did as unto the Lord. I would build every house as if the Lord Himself was going to live in it. I soon fell so in love with my job that I did not want to quit in the evenings. When I left the job at night I could not wait to get started the next day.

The job kept me busy and I could not think about the Lord all the time, but because I was doing everything for Him, I dwelt in His presence. Every day I left my job feeling as though I had been in a worship service! The job did not change; I changed. Even though I worked hard, the work refreshed me because it was a labor of love. It is never toil when we labor for the ones we love. Whatever our job is, if we will do it as worship unto Him, there will be a remarkable difference in our perspective on the job from that time on.

Just as a change in my heart was needed to turn drudgery into a glorious experience in carpentry, there have been times when I have turned the ministry into drudgery. Whether the diversion is rooted in a desire to promote my own ministry, or to do a personal favor for someone, or to gain money, or out of guilt—whenever I stop ministering out of a passion for the Lord and His truth and do it for any other reason, the ministry becomes a burden. If we take any other yoke than the Lord's, it will bring weariness and staleness to our ministry.

It is no accident that the Lord instituted the Sabbath when He gave Israel the manna from heaven. It is only as we abide in Him and His rest that our manna can be gathered fresh every day. Neither our life, nor our work, nor our ministry need ever become stale. If they do, we need to examine whose yoke we are wearing. If we are yoked with the Lord, we will always be refreshed by our labors, regardless of what they are.

Chapter 16

RESTORATION

AND

REDEMPTION

We were created *by* the Son and *for* the Son (Colossians 1:16) and in His image (Genesis 1:26). This sums up the ultimate purpose of the creation.

When we determined to live for ourselves instead of for God, we marred the image in which we were created. Our whole purpose now is to be restored to the image of the Son. That process is called *restoration*, which includes *redemption*. We must understand this if we are going to cease from our own labors and enter into what God has already accomplished.

In the first sermon preached on the first day of the church's birth, Peter summed up restoration in one brief statement:

> **Repent therefore and return, that your sins may be wiped away, in order that times of refreshing may come from the presence of the Lord;**
>
> **and that He may send Jesus, the Christ appointed for you,**
>
> **whom heaven must receive until the *period of restoration of all things* about which God spoke by the mouth of His holy prophets from ancient time (Acts 3:19-21).**

It is a part of God's ultimate intention to *restore all things*. What does this mean? To comprehend this, we must grasp the overview of the whole story of the Bible.

The first two and last two chapters of the Bible constitute a complete story. In Genesis 1, man has a position and relationship with God that is unique in the creation. In chapter three, man loses that position and relationship because of his rebellion.

The entire remainder of the Bible, except for its last two chapters, is devoted to *restoring* man to the position and relationship which he lost. In the last two chapters of the Bible, man's restoration has been completed. In Revelation 21 and 22, John sees a new heaven and a new earth, where fellowship with God has been reestablished and **"the old order of things has passed away" (Revelation 21:4 NIV).**

The following chart illustrates the main points of man's separation and restoration:

Separation and Restoration

Genesis 1	Revelation 21
God walks with man and has intimate fellowship with him.	The fellowship is restored and God again dwells with man.
Genesis 3	**Revelation 20**
Man is seduced by the serpent and Satan is released on the earth to take the dominion that was man's rightful place.	Satan is bound and Jesus, the last Adam, sets up His throne on the earth.
Genesis 3	**Revelation 22**
Man is driven from the garden so that he cannot eat of the Tree of Life.	Man is *restored* to the Tree of Life.
Genesis 3	**Revelation 21**
The earth is cursed.	The curse is removed and there is no more mourning, crying or pain.
Genesis 3	**Revelation 20 & 21**
Death enters the world and everything living on earth must suffer it.	"Death & Hades" are thrown into the lake of fire; there is a new heaven and a new earth in which there is no more death.

Fellowship Is the Goal

The first privilege that was lost by the fall was fellowship with God. Regaining that fellowship is the first main goal of restoration. This is the purpose of redemption and should be the first and main goal in the life of every redeemed soul. Our first calling is to fellowship with the One who has redeemed us (I Corinthians 1:9). This is the first priority of true Christianity and the primary issue that distinguishes Christianity from all other religions. Christianity is not just a formula for moral living. *True Christianity is the restoration of union with God.*

True Christianity is being born again by God's Spirit. This rebirth initiates the process of restoring our union with Him. The new birth is a new *beginning*, not an ending. It is but the *first* step in our restoration process. True Christianity is a journey to intimate fellowship with our Father. If Christian maturity can be measured at all, it would have to be measured in relation to our intimacy with Him.

When we begin to measure our spiritual stature by how long we have been Christians, by how much knowledge we have, or even by our acts of faith, it is only a reflection of the fact that we have somehow departed from the course. The issue of faith is not how much we know *about* God—it is how close we are to Him.

The Greek word most often translated "fellowship" in the New Testament is *koinonia*. It literally means "communion." Our word *communion* was originally two words, "common" and "union," that were merged to form one word. To say people have something "in common" speaks of their being like one another or having a union of purpose. Both of these meanings relate to the nature of our union with God. Through our fellowship with God, we become like Him and we have a common purpose with Him.

Most of us have noticed elderly couples who have been together for so many years that they have begun to look alike. It is a remarkable phenomenon. Just being with someone over a period of time will make us like them, both in mannerisms and, in a strange way, even in appearance.

So too, we are changed into the Lord's image—simply by being with Him. **"But we all, with unveiled face beholding as in a mirror the glory of the Lord, are being transformed into the same image from glory to glory, just as from the Lord, the Spirit" (II Corinthians 3:18).** It is as we behold the Lord that we are changed into His image. *We do not change so that we can fellowship with Him; we are changed by our fellowship with Him.*

Doing the Works of God

Our first calling is to fellowship, not works. When we forget this, we will begin to distort the character of true Christianity. God's rest is not just for the purpose of rejuvenation; it is for finding God and abiding in Him. Jesus simply abided in the Father and the Father did His works through Him. As He explained: **"The Father abiding in Me does His works" (John 14:10).** Though He felt compassion for the human condition, *Jesus never responded to human need; He only responded to what He saw the Father doing.*

In this same way, we are to abide in Jesus. We cannot do the works of God apart from God. Paul explained to the men of Athens, **"The God who made the world and all things in it...does not dwell in temples made with hands; neither is He served by human hands"** (Acts 17:24-25). Only the Spirit can beget that which is Spirit. The primary reason for "burnout" in ministry today is our tendency to take the people's yokes instead of the Lord's yoke. The Lord Himself entreated us:

> **Come to Me, all who are weary and heavy-laden, and I will give you rest.**
>
> **Take My yoke upon you, and learn from Me, for I am gentle and humble in heart; and you shall find rest for your souls.**
>
> **For My yoke is easy, and My load is light (Matthew 11:28-30).**

If we are carrying a heavy load, it is because we have taken up a yoke that is not the Lord's. Weariness in our work is a sure sign that we have not been abiding in Him. Although a yoke is given to enable work to be done, when we are yoked with the Lord, He does the work through us. When we work with Him, rather than becoming depleted, we actually find rest. If we would refuse the yokes of human expectations that are put on most ministries, the people would receive far more true ministry than they do now.

Because of his fall, the ground where man lived and worked was cursed. It then followed that, **"In toil you shall eat of it...By the sweat of your face you shall eat bread"** **(Genesis 3:17,19).** There is a difference between toil and labor. Toil is a curse, but labor is not. Man labored (cultivated) in the garden before the fall (Genesis 2:15). Toil is defined as "accomplishing *with great and painful effort,"* or *"to advance with difficulty."* The curse of toil is removed in Christ, but we still labor.

When we attempt spiritual labor without entering God's rest, it is like driving a car that is stuck in the sand. We may have a two hundred horsepower motor putting out all that it has, but we will not go anywhere. Those who do not know the rest of God will substitute activity and energy for advancement. Regardless of how many temples they may build with human hands, spiritually they are still stuck in the sand.

In Jeremiah 50:6 the Lord makes an even more sobering declaration:

> **My people have become lost sheep;**
> **Their shepherds have led them astray.**
> **They have made them turn aside on the mountains;**
> **They have gone along from mountain to hill**
> **And** *have forgotten their resting place.*

Many Christians who are led astray are deceived in this same way. Their shepherds are taking them from mountain to hill, from one thing that pumps them up to the next, from hype to hype. But they are not being led to their resting place—to the Lord of the Sabbath Himself.

This is certainly one of the primary causes of the Laodicean lukewarmness in the church today. The people are simply worn out from all the projects and hype, things which will never satisfy their souls. If we who are shepherds are not leading God's people to His rest, we are guilty of leading them astray.

The Lord is still exhorting us, **"Cease striving and know that I am God" (Psalm 46:10).** If we really know that He is God, we will cease striving. God holds the universe in His hand. He is able to accomplish His purposes in us. We only strive because we worry, and worry is the opposite of faith. If we really believe that He is God and in control, how can we worry? When we *really* believe that He is God, we will rest in Him. When we strive, it is because we have lost sight of Who He is.

> **"Today if you hear His voice,**
> **Do not harden your hearts as when they provoked Me,**
> **As in the day of trial in the wilderness...**
>
> **"Therefore I was angry with this generation,**
> **And said, 'They always go astray in their heart;**
> **And they did not know My ways';**
>
> **As I swore in My wrath,**
> **'They shall not enter My rest'" (Hebrews 3:7-8, 10-11).**

Here He says, **"They always go astray *in their heart*...they did not know My ways...they shall not enter My rest."** Just believing in our minds does not accomplish anything unless that knowledge is transferred to our hearts. That transfer from head to heart is always reflected in how we live—especially by how we live when we are under pressure or in the midst of trials. The Lord said, **"They always go astray in their *heart*,"** *not their mind*.

As Christians, we have usually been zealous to challenge each other as to *what* we believe, but God is more interested in *how* we believe. When we go astray, the problem is almost always a matter of our heart rather than our mind. We can accurately believe all the right doctrines, yet not live any of them. We can have the whole Bible memorized, and yet be rebels. Many of us believe God in our minds but not in our hearts, **"For with the *heart* man believes, resulting in righteousness" (Romans 10:10).**

When we come before the judgment seat of Christ, He will not be examining our doctrinal statements. If we love the truth, we will want to have accurate doctrine, but accurate doctrines will do us no good if we do not live them and if we are not being changed into the image of Christ.

Knowing God's Ways

The Lord said, **"They did not know My ways...they shall not enter My rest."** *Knowing God's ways leads to His rest.* David wrote, **"He made known His ways to Moses, His acts to the sons of Israel" (Psalm 103:7).**

Moses was one of the most spiritually discerning men to ever live. When the Lord determined to destroy Israel for their rebellion, Moses had the confidence to stand between the Lord and the people and intercede for their lives. When the plague began to sweep through the camp, Moses knew exactly how to stop it. He sent Aaron with a censor of incense, a type of prayer and intercession. **"So he put on the incense and made atonement for the people. And he took his stand between the dead and the living, so that the plague was checked" (Numbers 16:47-48).**

This was an unprecedented act. There were no laws that said incense would stop plagues. Moses intuitively knew what to do because he knew God's ways. Knowledge of principles and formulas is not what makes men into decisive spiritual leaders; true leaders are those who know God and His ways. In Exodus 33:12-18 we see the constitution of Moses' heart, the key to his great discernment:

> **Then Moses said to the LORD, "See, Thou dost say to me, 'Bring up this people!' But Thou Thyself has not let me know whom Thou wilt send with me. Moreover, Thou hast said, 'I have known you by name, and you have also found favor in My sight.'**
>
> **"Now therefore, I pray Thee, if I have found favor in Thy sight, let me know Thy ways, that I may know Thee, so that I may find favor in Thy sight. Consider too, that this nation is Thy people."**

And He said, "My presence shall go with you, and I will give you rest."

Then he [Moses] said to Him, "If Thy presence does not go with us, do not lead us up from here.

For how then can it be known that I have found favor in Thy sight, I and Thy people? Is it not by *Thy going with us*, so that we, I and Thy people, may be *distinguished from all the other people who are upon the face of the earth?*"

And the LORD said to Moses, "I will also do this thing of which you have spoken; for you have found favor in My sight, and I have known you by name."

Then Moses said, "I pray Thee, show me Thy glory!" (Exodus 33:12-18)

Moses' great wisdom was in understanding that if the Lord's presence did not go with them, he did not want to lead them any further. It is only by the presence of the Lord with us that the church is going to be distinguishable from any other group or religion that claims to follow God. Even if we have all the right doctrines about God, it will do us little good if we do not have *Him*! A distinguishing characteristic between true spiritual leaders versus pretenders is that true leaders have the wisdom not to proceed unless God is present with them.

Chapter 17

WATER FROM THE ROCK

For I do not want you to be unaware, brethren, that our fathers were all under the cloud, and all passed through the sea;

and all were baptized into Moses in the cloud and in the sea;

and all ate the same spiritual food;

and all drank the same spiritual drink, for they were drinking from a spiritual rock which followed them; *and the rock was Christ* (I Corinthians 10:1-4).

A rock followed Israel during her wilderness journey and *"the rock was Christ."* He was also the manna. Jesus is the Source of the true Bread and Water of life. In the wilderness we learn this and become utterly dependent on Him. We learn to both hunger and thirst for Him. It is only the water which issues from the presence of the Lord Himself which can quench the true thirst of the human soul.

Plants and animals have different forms of food, but every living thing must have water in basically the same form. This is a revelation of Christ that is seldom understood. The creation is not God, as the pantheists proclaim, but the creation does express the Lord and His nature. We do not worship nature, but we do look at it to *clearly see* God's attributes, eternal power and divine nature, as Paul explained:

For since the creation of the world His invisible attributes, His eternal power and divine nature, have been *clearly seen*, being understood through what has been made, so that they are without excuse (Romans 1:20).

For by Him all things were created, both in the heavens and on earth, visible and invisible, whether thrones or dominions or rulers or authorities—all things have been created by Him and for Him.

And He is before all things, and in Him all things hold together (Colossians 1:16-17).

A healthy human being can usually go forty days without food, but no one can go more than a few days without water. The manna represented Jesus as the fresh revelation and understanding of God that we need to receive daily. The water speaks of Him in a much more profound sense.

Paul explained, **"in him we live, and move, and have our being" (Acts 17:28 KJV).** Jesus is the fundamental Reason for the universe and for everything that was created. The whole creation reflects Christ. He is the "Living Water." Just as over seventy percent of the earth's surface is water and over seventy percent of nearly every living thing is composed of water, the Lord fills all that live and holds them together. He is not the creation, but He does permeate the creation with His presence.

If Christ were removed from the world, everything living would immediately die and collapse into dust. Even the atheists who do not believe in Him could not exist for a single second without Him! **"In Him all things hold together."**

This is the way in which a special presence and grace of the Lord so permeates the universe that we often do not recognize Him, and even if we do, we most likely take Him for granted. Every human being partakes of the presence of the Lord every day whether he realizes it or not. This is the common grace that God gives to all men. He allows His sun (Son) to shine on both the just and the unjust.

Elizabeth Browning once stated, "Earth is crammed with heaven, and every bush is aflame with the glory of God. But only those who see take off their shoes; the rest just pick the berries." The special presence of Christ upholds the universe.

If we would open our eyes, we would see Him in everything and continually partake of the pure Water of Life.

If we had awakened this morning and turned over to find Jesus Himself standing next to our bed, most of us would have had a much different day! The truth is that when we arose this morning, Jesus was there. If the eyes of our hearts had been open, we would have seen Him, and we would have continued to see Him clearly all day long. We must learn to recognize the Rock that follows us, the One Who is the Source of all living water.

The creation is not God, but He is reflected in the creation just as the artist is reflected in all of his works. By studying his works we can, to a degree, understand the artist. But how much better could we get to know an artist if we could meet him personally and spend time with him?

The same is true of the Lord. There is much we can learn about His character and His ways by observing His creation, and this is a wonderful thing to do. But we also have direct access to the Lord Himself at any time. Let us never forget the best part! Instead of studying the creation to find Him or understand Him, let us study His creation *with Him.*

Although **"the glory of kings is to search out a matter" (Proverbs 25:2),** it is wisdom to understand that our revelation of God must come from Him. We can never come to the knowledge of His ways by our own efforts because His ways are higher than our ways and His thoughts are higher than our thoughts (Isaiah 55:8-9). What we can give to the

Lord is our devotion and our seeking hearts. If we seek Him, we will find Him. If we knock, He will open the door. If we ask, we will receive.

There is nothing in this universe more valuable or desirable than the Lord Himself, and He has made Himself readily available to us. The Rock which follows us is not just a stone—it is Christ. Let us take every advantage of our wilderness experiences to learn to draw water from the Rock.

Smiting the Rock

There were two incidents when Moses was commanded to draw water from the rock. The first is recorded in Exodus 17 and the other in Numbers 20. The first time Moses was commanded to take his rod and strike the rock. This act was a prophetic type showing that Christ would be smitten for our sins in order to bring forth the living waters for the congregation of God.

The second time Moses was told to **"speak to the rock" (Numbers 20:8).** Out of his frustration with the people, he struck the rock a second time. Because of his disobedience in striking the rock a second time instead of speaking to it as he was commanded, Moses was not allowed to enter into the Promised Land. These two incidents involving Moses, the rock, and water for the people illustrate a most poignant and relevant lesson for all who are called to walk in spiritual leadership.

Jesus was to be struck once and only once for our sins. This is clearly stated in Hebrews: **"Nor was it that He should offer Himself often...so Christ also, having been offered** *once* **to bear the sins of many, shall appear a second time for salvation" (Hebrews 9:25, 28).** Christ was to suffer only one time for our sins; after that He is never to be struck again. If we use our rod of authority to strike the Head and make demands of Him, we have fallen into a most terrible presumption that could also cost us that which we have been promised.

When we use our spiritual authority against the Lord we are, like Moses, treading on very dangerous ground. Some of the greatest tragedies in recent church history have resulted from men of God trying to use the Word of God to strike Him. They use God's Word to demand His compliance and submission. Such action is not faith in the Word; it is presumption in a most deadly form.

As with Moses, we are most often pressed to take rash actions by the pressure of our frustration with immature or rebellious people. When we are given authority from God, we must be careful how we use it. We must never use our spiritual authority out of frustration. God's authority is only for use in obedience to the Holy Spirit, who does not get frustrated. Patience is His nature. Many men and women of God have failed to walk in the fullness of what they were called to because they have wrongly used their God-given authority.

The Lord is full of grace and truth, and we live in the age of grace, no longer under the law. Moses, who had instituted the law, was bound to pay the price for his transgression while we can approach the throne of grace. Few who have walked in spiritual authority have been perfect in their exercise of that authority. Most of us have used it improperly many times, often not even aware that we have. Even so, the higher the level of authority, the greater the consequences for our misuse of that authority.

If one of Israel's elders had made the same mistake Moses did, it is probable that God would have given him no more than a rebuke. However, when we walk in the higher levels of authority, we cannot get away with what we could at the lower levels. The more authority and influence we have, the more damage that can come from our misuse of authority. Greater spiritual authority requires a higher standard of obedience. What the Levites were allowed to get away with in the Outer Court could result in death for those serving in the Holy Place.

Two fundamental truths emerging from the Reformation were the priesthood of all believers and the realization that there is only one mediator between God and men, the man Christ Jesus. Nevertheless, there is a scriptural mandate for leaders in the New Covenant church to live by higher standards than may be tolerable to members of the general congregation. This is not a departure from the basic Reformation truths, or an attempt to further separate the clergy from the laity; it is simply a recognition that with greater spiritual authority comes greater responsibility.

The Jerusalem Council established that the only restraint put upon the believers was to **"abstain from things sacrificed to idols and from blood and from things strangled and from fornication;** *if you keep yourselves free from such things you will do well"* **(Acts 15:29).** Yet the letters of these apostles call to much higher standards those who would be deacons or elders. Again, the more spiritual authority we are called to carry, the more obedient we must be, for our own sake as well as the people.

It is remarkable that the Lord continues to entrust the kind of awesome power and authority that He does to men. But the fact that He does is not a reason for us to be presumptuous. Our God is holy; we must treat Him as holy. Notice the Lord's rebuke to Moses after he struck the rock a second time: **"Because you have not believed Me, to treat Me as holy in the sight of the sons of Israel, therefore you shall not bring this assembly into the land which I have given them" (Numbers 20:12).** Regardless of how much authority God has given to us, we must never be presumptuous with how we use it.

One of the great tragedies of church history is the number of men and women of God who, like Moses, serve the Lord so well and for so long, only to stumble and fall near the end of their lives. In most of these cases, there is at least a subtle pride in their accomplishments that leads these leaders to use the anointing of God for presumptuous or selfish reasons. The greater the person's anointing and visibility, the greater their fall has inevitably been.

To be an elder in the time of the early church was a noble thing. This was almost certainly a risk of one's life, and probably the lives of one's family members as well. In the modern Western church, elders often have more in common with corporate executives than they do with their biblical counterparts. How many positions of spiritual authority have we given away to honor a person, rather than requiring evidence of a clear call from God? Often men who were not prepared have been thrust into a most dangerous position. The result is that spiritual authority is tragically misused to the injury of many.

We have been entrusted with the care of God's own children. Woe to anyone who treats this responsibility with presumption or slothfulness. We will give an account! When Adam fell, billions would pay the price. When King David numbered the people, who paid the price for his transgression? The people! We may say that this is unfair, but there could be no true authority without responsibility. If we misuse our authority, it will hurt others. And the more authority that we have, the greater the number of those who will be hurt.

Those who seek position and visibility in the body of Christ do not realize that every bit of influence gained by any means other than the Holy Spirit will be a stumbling block to them. Anyone who understands spiritual authority will, like Christ, seek to become of no reputation rather than to make a reputation. He will seek to humble himself and become the servant of all rather than the leader of all. **"Whoever exalts**

himself shall be humbled; and whoever humbles himself shall be exalted" (Matthew 23:12). The degree to which we gain influence by any means other than by the promotion of the Holy Spirit will almost certainly be the degree to which we will ultimately be humiliated.

The wise leader will seek to walk in increasing humility, not increasing visibility. But let us not confuse humility with insecurity. When Moses was first called by the Lord he felt inadequate for the task. We often think that this is a humility that pleases God, but it is in fact a terrible presumption! Feelings of inadequacy are not humility; they are a manifestation of our continued self-centeredness.

The Pride of Inadequacy

It was said of Moses that he was the most humble man on the face of the earth (Numbers 12:3). Did you ever think about who wrote that? Moses did! Humility is not an inferiority complex—true humility is simple agreement with God. It was in true humility that Paul defended his apostleship, even when he declared that he labored more than any of the others. It can be pride and delusion for us to declare ourselves a prophet; it can also be pride and delusion for us not to! The whole issue is: *What has God said?*

When we declare ourselves inadequate for something God has called us to, we are basically saying that our inadequacy is greater than God's adequacy. We are also really saying that the task depends on our ability instead of God's. The anger of the Lord burned against Moses for this false humility.

We will never be adequate for a task that God has called us to. In fact, we will probably become dangerous if we start to *feel* adequate for what we are called to. We will always be inadequate for the work of God, and will therefore always be dependent on Him for His grace, power and authority. If you intend to wait until you feel adequate for the work before you enter the ministry, you will never fulfill your calling.

When God commanded Moses to cast down his rod, the symbol of his authority, it turned into a serpent and chased Moses until he picked it up again! The same will happen to us if we refuse the authority God has called us to. That is why Paul proclaimed, **"Woe is me if I do not preach the gospel"** **(I Corinthians 9:16).** But when we pick up the authority that God has called us to, even if we have not promoted ourselves and all our authority really was received from Him, we can still become presumptuous or careless and misuse it. **"Therefore let him who thinks he stands take heed lest he fall" (I Corinthians 10:12).**

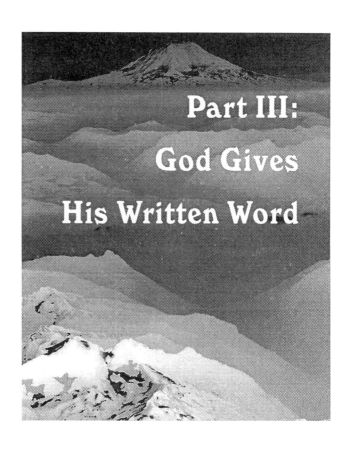

Part III:

God Gives

His Written Word

Chapter 18

THE WORD
MUST BECOME
FLESH

On Mount Sinai, God wrote the Ten Commandments in stone by His own hand. He then gave them to Moses to give to the people. This was the first installment of His gift to man in the written Word. First the Word was given as the Law. The Law was written in stone to symbolize its hard, rigid nature. The Law was given to reveal our hardness of heart.

But God's ultimate purpose for His Word was that it might become flesh. The Word first became flesh in Jesus. He made it possible for the Word to be made flesh in all of us. The Word is made flesh in us when it is changed from being just concepts and principles to being our very nature. Then it will not just be what we believe, but who we are.

The apostolic task was more than just getting the people to believe the right doctrines, it was to labor until Christ, the Word of God, was formed *in* His people. The apostolic mandate was not one of conformation but of formation. Humanism seeks to change the nature of man by changing his environment, institutions, governments and rules of behavior. Christianity changes the institutions, governments, and behavior of men by changing their hearts. The ultimate purpose of the Word of God is not just to get us to believe and do the right things, but to get us to believe and do the right things for the right reasons—because we love God and are united with His purposes.

God called Moses to climb the mountain into His presence in order to receive His Word. For the next four thousand years, other individuals were likewise called into His presence and given God's Word for mankind. These words are more valuable than all the treasures that have ever been mined on earth; these are treasures that have been mined in heaven. Having been ultimately compiled into one book, the Bible points the way to the bridge between heaven and earth, so that we may all ascend into His presence.

Jesus Is the Word

"In the beginning was the Word, and the Word was with God, and the Word was God" (John 1:1). Jesus is the Word of God personified. The written Word is the revelation of Jesus, His will and His plan for mankind. Again, God's ultimate purpose is for all things to be summed up in His Son

(Ephesians 1:10). The written Word of God is given to lead us to Him. It is an expression of Jesus, and Jesus is the expression of the written Word made flesh in man. These two things, Jesus and the Word, are not separate but are a complete revelation of the will and heart of God for us.

Our ability to properly understand the Bible will be a primary factor in our ability to partake of the Bread of Life and to be the light that God has called us to be. This statement is made with the understanding that many of the great pillars of the faith, both historically and presently, who stood uncompromisingly for the truth against the most cruel and terrible opposition, had little or no access to a Bible. Even though many of these from the persecuted church may not have had a Bible, they had the Author Himself living within them, just as we do. But those who have the Bible have been given much. **"From everyone who has been given much shall much be required" (Luke 12:48).**

The Bible is a gift from God of incomprehensible value. The Bible is given to help direct our life in Christ, to help keep us on the course, and to give us insight into the mind and heart of God. All of this is so that we might be changed into His same image. If we really esteem the Bible as God's Word, we will certainly handle it with the utmost care, yet we will be utterly free to partake of its content.

As Pharaoh was one of the great biblical models of Satan, Pharaoh's primary purpose was the same as Satan's continuing motive: to keep God's people in bondage. Moses is one of the great biblical types of Christ. Jesus has come to set us free from slavery and lead us to our Promised Land, just as Moses did with the Israelites. The basic dichotomy between the kingdom of God and this present evil age that lies in the power of the evil one is the issue of freedom versus slavery.

Satan knows that we cannot truly serve God until we are free. **"Where the Spirit of the Lord is, there is liberty" (II Corinthians 3:17).** We cannot receive the true substance and power of the written Word of God until there is the freedom of spirit to receive it into our innermost being, not just in our minds. That is why freedom of conscience and freedom of religion are the most precious freedoms of all.

The Revolutionary Power of the Word

When Jesus was asked by John's disciples whether He was indeed the "Expected One," the evidence He gave of His ministry as proof included the fact that **"the poor have the gospel preached to them" (Luke 7:22).**

God's heart has always gone out to the poor and the oppressed, but there is a strategic reason for this as well. Great social changes have never taken place until the common people were moved by the truth. It is no accident that when the Bible was finally translated into the languages of the common people, democracy and free enterprise were the immediate result. The Lord was not trying to change our forms of government and economy; the changes that occurred were simply the result of people becoming spiritually free.

The primary spiritual and historic battleground in the conflict between freedom and slavery has been fought over the Bible. When the Bible is preached, the people are set free from the yokes of the evil one, and a return to fellowship with and obedience to God is the result. Satan's primary strategy during the Middle Ages was to keep the Bible out of the hands of the common people. Anyone who was caught with a Bible was put to death.

When the Bible was read to the people by the religious establishment during that time, it was read only in the archaic Latin language which most of the people could not understand. This resulted in "The Dark Ages," the period of the greatest human depravity yet recorded in history. When the enemy lost the battle to keep the Bible out of the hands of the common people, he devised other strategies to keep people from reading and understanding it.

It was the doctrine of the ecclesiastical authorities in the Middle Ages that only the spiritual professionals, the priests, had the wisdom and scholarship to properly interpret the Word. They argued that if the common people tried to interpret the Bible they would only fall into heresy.

There is some truth to what they said. There is indeed a danger in promoting the freedom of individuals to interpret the Scriptures for themselves, because some people will fall into heresy. *But there is a far greater danger if we do not allow people this freedom!* The truth is that the most diabolical doctrines ever promoted originated at times when only the chosen spiritual professionals had access to the Word of God.

The Gnostics

One of the primary doctrinal conflicts in the early church was with the Gnostics. The Gnostics promoted the belief that there was a hidden message in the Bible that only the initiated elite could understand. Although some of their heretical doctrines were rightly removed from the church, the basic premise of Gnosticism took control of the institutional church. In the conflict over the Bible, this subtle form of Gnosticism has been Satan's heavy artillery.

The Gnostic spirit has crept into almost every Christian movement and denomination to some degree, but its primary strongholds have actually been in the "ultra" conservative and the "ultra" liberal camps of the Catholic, Protestant and Evangelical churches. This is not to imply that all conservatives are motivated by this diabolical snare. However, the extremists of almost every sectarian camp usually are. The breeding ground of Gnosticism is extremism founded upon pride and elitism. The primary goal of Gnosticism is to remove the Word of God from the common people, who are the most dangerous to the enemy once they perceive truth.

The wealthy and the politically powerful are rarely able to even see the truth through the thick veil of their own self-interests. When they do see it, they can seldom respond to it because of their many earthly entanglements. The poor, the weak and the oppressed usually have nothing to lose by radically responding to the truth, and they usually will.

With prophetic power that has not been equaled since, Martin Luther, a lowly German monk who would not compromise his convictions, nailed his Ninety-five Thesis to the little Wittenburg church door—and the whole world changed! The most fearful sight to the camp of the enemy is the Word of God in the hands of a humble man who will not compromise his convictions.

Such integrity is seldom found except in the common man. When the poor have the gospel preached to them, the world is going to change. Once Satan lost the battle to keep the Bible from being printed and given to the poor, his next strategy was to make the poor believe that they could not understand it. Once the Bible was in the hands of the people, the next battleground was to keep *interpretation* out of their minds and hearts.

It is true that there are mysteries and hidden meanings in the Scriptures that cannot be understood without Divine enlightenment. Gnosticism claims that God gives His enlightenment only to the elite. The truth is that God *does* give His revelation only to the select, but they are the humble, not the elite. Only the humble will be free from the self-interests and agendas that veil the truth from the proud. Only the humble have so little to lose that they are willing to obey the truth.

Obedience to the truth is the key to unlocking the meaning of the Scriptures. As Jesus Himself declared, **"If any man is *willing to do His will*, he shall know of the teaching, whether it is of God, or whether I speak from Myself"** (John 7:17). The willingness to uncompromisingly obey the Word of God is what separates those who can properly understand His teaching from those who cannot.

Intolerance and Pharisaism

The Pharisees loved and esteemed the Scriptures more than anyone else. Because of this devotion, they were given the primary responsibility for maintaining the integrity of the Scriptures through centuries of copying and recopying. For this, we do owe them much.

Sadly, though, in their zeal for protecting the Scriptures, the Pharisees implemented a system of scriptural interpretation based on their traditions rather than the humility of seeking the Lord for interpretation. Their web of traditions caused them to miss, and even persecute, the One who personified the very Word of God.

Today there are ultraconservative camps of Christianity in which modern Pharisees are doing the same thing. In their zeal to protect the Scriptures from doctrinal abuse, these modern Pharisees have erected a reactionary system of interpretation which actually works to prohibit people from perceiving truth.

Everyone who loves the truth wants to have accurate doctrine. Even so, accurate doctrines are a means, not the end. By them we determine the will of God so that we can obey Him. We can have the Bible memorized, yet still not obey the Lord. The Pharisees loved the Scriptures more than they loved the God of the Scriptures, and many today fall into this same trap. We cannot love God without loving His Word, but we must not make an idol out of the Scriptures that actually eclipses our love for Him.

Even after losing the battle to keep the Bible out of the hands of the common people, Satan has continued to enslave much of the church through "spiritual totalitarianism." By this I mean that he controls and oppresses people through fear and intimidation. Satan knows very well that, **"with the heart man believes, resulting in righteousness" (Romans 10:10).**

Fear and intimidation can pressure us into believing with our minds, but it will never reach our hearts. Intimidation and fear will never result in true faith. Fear is the counter power to faith. Fear is the power of the kingdom of darkness; it enslaves. Faith is the power of the kingdom of God that sets us free to worship God in Spirit and truth. Fear rules man through external pressure and intimidation; faith rules from the heart.

A parrot can be taught to say and do the right things, but it will not be in his heart. When we believe something because we are intimidated or pressured into believing it, our belief will never result in true righteousness, regardless of how accurate or true it is. Satan cares little about what we believe as long as it is a mere intellectual understanding. True "living waters" can come only from the innermost being. We will never be able to teach or preach that which imparts true life until we preach from our hearts.

The basic conflict is still between slavery and freedom. Jesus said, **"If you abide in My word, then you are truly disciples of Mine; and** *you shall know the truth, and the truth shall make you free"* **(John 8:31-32).** The truth makes us free, and it is freedom that enables us to comprehend the truth. Obedience to God is important, but God is not *just* after obedience. He wants us to obey for the right reasons.

For example, some women wear hats to church as a symbol of their submission to authority. Wearing the hat is not the submission, but is rather a symbol of it. A rebellious woman may wear a hat, but that will not make her submissive. In fact, a rebellious woman might wear a hat in an attempt to disguise her *lack* of submission.

The Lord does not ask us to wear the symbols of our submission. He is looking for submission from the heart. Too many of the doctrines promulgated in Christianity put more emphasis on the wearing of doctrinal "hats" than on making changes in our hearts.

The Nature of Obedience

If all God required from man was obedience, He would not have given a choice to Adam and Eve in the garden. He did not put the Tree of Knowledge in the garden as a temptation. At the same point where they could choose to disobey Him was also the only point where they could *choose to obey* Him. If God had wanted only absolute obedience, He could have created Adam and Eve so they could not disobey Him. But He did not even create the angels that way. What good is worship from a thing that cannot do otherwise?

For there to be the potential for obedience from the heart, God had to give us a choice. The greater the choice, the greater the potential for choosing wrongly, and yet the greater the heart obedience toward God in those who choose correctly. However, if we erect walls around ourselves so that we cannot disobey, it will not produce a righteous heart. If a thief is put in jail he may not be able to steal, but that does not mean that stealing has been removed from his heart. When we erect walls and barriers around our doctrines through fear and intimidation like the Pharisees did, then we are only creating spiritual robots who may say and do all the right things, but who will never worship from their hearts.

Freedom is a prerequisite for a true relationship. Just as the Pharisees were the most devoted to the Scriptures, but were the greatest enemy of the Word Himself, many of those who are most outwardly devoted to protecting the integrity of the Word are the greatest enemies of the truth today. The modern Pharisees who work through fear and intimidation are the arch enemies of truth.

Those who are controlled by fear will be the most threatened by anyone they cannot control by intimidation. People who believe God with their hearts know the One in whom they believe. When we know that we are known by God, we will not be overly concerned about what anyone else thinks of us. Therefore, we will not be threatened or intimidated by anyone on earth. Those with this constitution will choose because it is right and not out of political pressure.

Jesus was tolerant of sinners, but had little tolerance for the Pharisees and doctors of the law. These were not entering the kingdom and would not to allow others to enter either. Modern Pharisees perceive those who deviate even a little from their rigid doctrines as enemies, false teachers or false prophets.

There are, of course, some false teachers and false prophets. However, these labels need only be applied to those whose teachings and practices undermine foundational doctrines, such as the atonement, grace or the nature of Christ. The apostles to the early church were more concerned about the **"false brethren who had sneaked in to spy out our liberty which we have in Christ Jesus, in order to bring us into bondage" (Galatians 2:4).**

Like the first century, these modern Pharisees are doing far more damage to the church than all the cults, false teachers and false prophets combined. In fact, they themselves are the ones that Scripture most identifies as the false teachers and false prophets.

Liberty is essential to worship in Spirit and truth. If we are going to worship in Spirit and truth, we cannot compromise a believer's freedom to have differences in the nonessential doctrines and beliefs. Those who infringe upon this liberty are enemies of the truth, even if their stated intent is to protect the truth.

By God's design, we presently **"see through a glass, darkly" (I Corinthians 13:12 KJV).** Each is able to see but a part of the whole picture, and we will never see the whole picture until we learn to put our parts together. God's unity is not a unity of conformity but a unity of many diverse parts. True heart faith is evidenced by tolerance for those who are different, which is required if there is ever going to be a true unity of the heart.

Each Must Gather His Own Manna

When the children of Israel were given manna from heaven, each household had to gather its own supply. The same holds true for gathering heavenly manna. We cannot rely solely upon the leaders for our spiritual food.

This is not to belittle the importance of leaders and teachers who give themselves to the Word and the ministry. Just as the Levites were essential for ministering to the congregation of Israel, our leaders are essential today. But leaders cannot take on the duty of the individual or the individual household. There is a difference between the general teaching that should be provided by those devoted to the ministry of the Word and the daily bread from heaven which must be gathered by each household.

How can an untrained person go to the Bible for a fresh word from heaven without falling into error or false teaching? This is one of the most important issues which has faced God's people during the four thousand years since the written Word was first given to man. Since the Reformation began, one of Christianity's greatest struggles has been for the freedom of ordinary people to have access to and interpret the Scriptures for themselves.

Even those movements most devoted to Restoration or Renewal have all eventually developed systems and methods of interpreting the Scriptures (hermeneutics) which tend to take this ability out of the hands of the people and keep biblical interpretation solely in the hands of professionals. Most of these systems have been developed for the noble purpose of preventing heresy or errors. Unfortunately, the remedies have too often proven more harmful than the diseases they were designed to treat.

Chapter 19

HERMENEUTICAL PROBLEMS

"Hermeneutics" simply means a system or method of interpretation. There is a proper way to develop and use hermeneutics to understand the Scriptures, but in any system we develop we must guard against choking the ability of individuals to read and understand the Bible for themselves. Some of the most conservative denominational leaders have erected barriers to the ability of individuals to receive a fresh revelation or interpretation from the Scriptures. This is typically done in order to protect the denomination's predetermined interpretations.

Many of the doctrines and interpretations held by conservative teachers are true, but they are limited and partial. There is obviously much more to be understood from the Bible than we presently do. Many aspects of conservative hermeneutics prevent, or at least greatly discourage, the much-needed further exploration and understanding of the Scriptures.

One of the most extraordinary phenomenons in Christianity has been the ability of Christians to read identical translations of the Bible and yet arrive at widely divergent interpretations. Part of this is actually by God's design. Different parts of the body see different aspects of the truth, all of which must be put together to see the whole picture. Only mature Christians will see how the different truths fit together and compliment each other rather than conflict.

But there are also many different interpretations which are truly in conflict. This is due in part to the acceptance of several quite different biblical interpretations within large portions of the church. Though some of these methods of interpretation have elements that have gravitated to extremes, they all tend to have some validity and have at least some of their roots in biblical precedents.

With all its different theological camps, the church has become like the proverbial blind men and the elephant. The one who found the leg was sure the elephant was like a tree. The one who found the tail thought that the elephant was like a rope. The one who found its ear thought that the other two were both mistaken; the thing was like a great leaf. They were all partially right but totally wrong. They could never identify the elephant until they listened to each other and combined their understanding.

Even those who have adopted an extreme method of biblical interpretation almost always use some principles from the opposite camp. Usually they don't know it, or at least don't admit it. For example, the Bible itself gives many precedents which allow for both the literal and the allegorical methods of interpretation. Though these methods seem to be in conflict with each other, most Christians actually use both methods in the formation of their teachings and doctrines. Though both methods have been carried to extremes by some, both have at least some justification. Each must be used to properly understand the Bible.

Those who exclusively use just one method of interpretation have had to erect barriers to protect themselves from encroachment and to promote their method. These barriers have brought as much confusion and division to the church as any of the errors they are meant to protect us from. *There is a God-ordained ambiguity preventing the establishment of an absolute law or method of biblical interpretation. This ambiguity is designed to keep us dependent on the Holy Spirit to lead us to truth.* Many paradoxes in Scripture are there because the truth is found in the tension between the extremes. Only the Holy Spirit can enable us to discern such truth and keep us in the proper tension between the extremes that will otherwise cause us to depart from the course.

As the psalmist wisely declared, **"The SUM of Thy word is truth" (Psalm 119:160).** Each of us may have a part that is true, but it is not the whole *truth* until it is properly fitted together with the other parts. Understanding the different camps of biblical interpretation can help us to receive the good without stumbling over the bad. For this reason, we will take the time to make a cursory examination of the primary methods of biblical interpretation used in the church.

But first we will examine what I call "heart hermeneutics." These are the principles of character which the Scriptures teach are required for the reception of truth. Without these principles of character, even the most perfect principles of hermeneutics will not lead us to the truth or keep us on the path of life.

Chapter 20

HEART
HERMENEUTICS

There are general principles of biblical interpretation which can *help* (not guarantee) those who are sincerely seeking truth. They can help us to stay within the boundaries of scriptural perspective *and* be led by the Holy Spirit. Along with these principles, there are certain conditions of the heart which are biblically established essentials for walking in truth. I call these essentials "heart hermeneutics."

If our hearts are not right, the most perfect hermeneutics will not help us, and our interpretations will inevitably become truths used for evil, such as bringing division in the church. In this study we will examine both the heart conditions and the scripturally established general principles of biblical interpretation. The heart conditions and the principles generally overlap to some degree.

1. We must worship God, not facts about Him.

A fundamental prerequisite for properly interpreting the Bible is that we do not just seek to hear the words of the Lord, but the Word Himself. The Lord Jesus testified in John 5:39, **"You search the Scriptures, because you think that in them you have eternal life; and it is these that bear witness of Me."** *It is not enough to know the book of the Lord. We must know the Lord of the book.*

If we love the Lord, we will also love the Bible because it is His Word. If we love the truth, we will also be devoted to accuracy in biblical interpretation. If we do not properly esteem the Bible, we will eventually resort to using it to justify our own prejudices and ambitions. The Bible has been used to justify almost every heresy, but there is no fault in the Bible. The fault is in the self-centeredness and self-promotion which has motivated those who have used the Word of God for selfish reasons. A person who really loves the truth and the Word of God will not use the Word to justify his position. He is willing to learn from the Word, even when the Word proves him wrong. If we do not have this attitude, we love our self-esteem more than we love the truth.

2. Only the grace of humility can keep us in a proper balance between Pharisaism and fanaticism.

The straight and narrow path that leads to life (Matthew 7:13-14) is simply that—*straight and narrow.* To walk on a straight and narrow path, *balance* is needed. We can only maintain proper balance if we are led by the Spirit. Response to external pressures will almost certainly push us off course on one side or the other.

At times, the truth is found in what some, or even many, consider to be an extreme position. A position is not true simply because it is found between the extremes. Almost all prophetic voices in both Scripture and history were considered radicals and extremists in their day, even though later generations generally considered most of them to be moderates. These "radical" prophetic voices include the Lord Jesus and His apostles. Even today, they would not be easily received by many who claim to be the custodians of the true Word.

Walking in truth requires an extraordinary balance between resistance to change and addiction to change. Many non-traditionalists are nothing more than rebels against tradition, and rebellion does not lead us to truth. If Satan cannot stop us, he will try to push us to go too fast or too far. The Word without the Spirit will lead to Pharisaism; the Spirit without the Word will lead to fanaticism. It takes the proper balance of the Word and the Spirit to keep us on the path that leads to life. That path is narrow, and traps are laid for those who deviate from it.

How do we find the proper balance? Our typical Western mind set is to find a formula for it. In the case of biblical interpretation, however, formulas create a serious problem.

Formulas, even those based on wisdom and insight, will not be enough to keep us on the narrow path that leads to life. Remaining on the path of life depends on one basic factor—God's grace.

This does not imply that there is nothing we can do ourselves. On the contrary, there is much that we can do. The Lord made it clear that His grace can be appropriated through humility. **"God is opposed to the proud, but gives grace to the humble" (James 4:6).** In verse 10 the exhortation is to **"Humble yourselves."** Humbling ourselves is what *we* must do if we want to continue walking in truth. The spiritually mature would rather have the whole world count them as fools than have God count them as proud. They know that the opposition of God is to be feared far more than the opposition of all men and devils combined.

"Humble yourselves, therefore, under the mighty hand of God, that He may exalt you at the proper time" (I Peter 5:6). If we are devoted to humbling ourselves, God will devote Himself to lifting us up. If we are devoted to exalting ourselves, He will be devoted to humbling us.

The choice is ours. If we try to do His job, He will then do our job. We can be assured that He can do either one better than we can. Mature Christians must be devoted to seeking the lowest position, esteeming God's grace as more valuable than their reputation. Those who are devoted to lifting themselves up will always find themselves in a continuing and increasing battle to maintain their image and position because the Lord Himself will increase His opposition to them until they are humbled.

3. "Blessed are the pure in heart, for they shall see God" (Matthew 5:8).

To see the pure Word of God requires a pure heart. Any evil motives will distort what we see, even if we have the most perfect hermeneutics.

Self-seeking is a corrupting influence which hinders our ability to know the truth. The Lord Jesus made this clear when He said in John 7:18, **"He who speaks from himself seeks his own glory [literally, *recognition*]; but He who is seeking the glory of the one who sent Him, He is true, and there is no unrighteousness in Him."**

Once we realize how destructive self-seeking can be, most will then try to empty themselves. This too can lead to a departure from grace. The statement "we must decrease so that He can increase" is a misquotation of the Scripture. John said, *"He must increase,* **but I must decrease" (John 3:30).**

Having the correct order is important. If we decrease before He increases in our life we will get nothing but empty! As we seek the increase of Christ we *will* decrease. The gospel is **"yes"** and **"amen" (II Corinthians 1:19-20),** which means that it is positive, not negative. As we seek to glorify Jesus, we will see His glory and be changed by Him. A passion for the Son of God will displace the self-centeredness which has so crippled us.

One of the linchpin Scriptures of the New Testament is Galatians 2:20: *"I have been crucified with Christ*; **and it is no longer I who live, but Christ lives in me."** Our life is found when we are crucified with Him; if we try to crucify ourselves we will get nothing but self-righteousness, the most destructive form of pride that we can have. While we must learn to take up our crosses daily, this laying down of our lives is not primarily for the sake of changing us but for the sake of ministry to the world.

It is written that **"Enoch walked with God; and he was not, for God took him"** (Genesis 5:24). It was as Enoch walked with God that **"he was not."** He decreased until **"God took him."** This scripture speaks of Enoch's literal translation, but that is, in a sense, what we are referring to— being translated into the image of the Son of God.

This happens as we walk with God, not as we just sit around trying to get empty. As we seek the Lord's increase, we will decrease and hardly be aware of it. To concentrate on how empty we are getting is to continue in our self-centeredness, increasing the very demon we are seeking to cast out.

4. Love must be the goal of our study.

"The goal of our instruction is *love from a pure heart* **and a good conscience and a sincere faith"** (I Timothy 1:5). Those who love God from a pure heart can see God without distorting Him. The goal of all biblical studies must be to grow in love, not just in knowledge. We can want the truth for many wrong reasons: to prove ourselves worthy, to gain power and influence over others, or even to use in attacking others. When our motive for learning departs from growing in love and having a pure heart and sincere faith, we have drifted from the truth, or at least the proper use of it.

Jesus summed up all the "do nots" of the law in Matthew 22:37-40 when He said: **"You shall love the Lord your God with all your heart, and with all your soul, and with all your mind"** and **"You shall love your neighbor as yourself."** Love is the seed and genius of the New Covenant. He replaced all the negatives (the "do nots") of the Law with the simple positive of love. If we love, we will not do any of the negatives. If we love the Lord, we will not worship idols. If we love our neighbor, we will not envy him, murder him, etc. If we remain focused on the positives, we will automatically refrain from doing what we are forbidden to do.

5. Study to show yourselves approved unto God, not men (see II Timothy 2:15 KJV).

To the degree that we are subject to the fear of men, we destroy our ability to receive truth. The degree to which we seek human approval, or react to human disapproval, will be directly related to the degree to which we can perceive truth.

"The fear of man brings a snare" (Proverbs 29:25). In Galatians 1:10, Paul wrote, **"If I were still trying to please men, *I would not be a bond-servant of Christ."*** The Lord Jesus said, **"Woe to you when all men speak well of you, for in the**

same way their fathers used to treat the false prophets" (Luke 6:26).

When we study the Bible for any reason other than to know and obey God, we open the door for a subtle but profound distortion of the truth. The only way that we can really know the Word of God is by knowing God Himself. We will not know His Word fully until we know Him fully. The Lord declared: "**'For My thoughts are not your thoughts, neither are your ways My ways,' declares the LORD. 'For as the heavens are higher than the earth, so are My ways higher than your ways, and My thoughts than your thoughts'**" (Isaiah 55:8-9). As long as we are seeing from the human perspective, we will not understand God's thoughts or His ways.

6. We must keep our attention focused on the ultimate purpose of God, or we will be continually distracted by the lesser purposes of God.

Most of the extremes and distortions of biblical truth have resulted from our tendency to be distracted from the River of Life by the little tributaries which feed it. The complete purpose of God is to see all things conformed to the image of His Son. The apostolic vision had little to do with what form the church would take. Instead, the apostles were most concerned with *whose image* the church would bear. They did not labor to get the church to comply with certain forms, but as Paul declared, **"I am again in labor until Christ is formed** *in you"* **(Galatians 4:19).**

Paul also wrote, **"But I am afraid, lest as the serpent deceived Eve by his craftiness, your minds should be led astray from the simplicity and purity of devotion to Christ"** **(II Corinthians 11:3).** We will not be judged by how *much truth* we know, but by how *faithful* we are to the truth we know. A primary concern of the Father will be how much of the image of His Son we bear.

7. Truth is not given to us so that we can know, but so that we can become. When the fresh truths we perceive cease to change us, we have departed from the way.

The whole point of biblical truth is to help us become conformed to the image of Jesus Christ. As Thomas â Kempis declared, "I would rather *feel* contrition than just know the definition. What good does it do a man to be able to discourse profoundly concerning the Trinity if he is void of humility and thereby displeasing to the Trinity?"

8. We can only understand the eternal Word of God when we look at it from the perspective of eternity.

It is quite evident that the Word has practical applications for appropriating its power into our daily lives. Nevertheless, as with Abraham, we will not be able to walk in a day by day faith until we can also see the promises "from afar off."

In Hebrews 11, which is popularly referred to as "the faith chapter," there is a long list of faithful saints who received extraordinary deliverances or attained great promises. This is an important aspect of faith: We must be able to appropriate the power and life of God into our own lives if it is to be real. But there is another group in that list that is seldom mentioned—those who **"were tortured,** *not accepting their release, in order that they might obtain a better resurrection"* **(verse 35).**

The implication of this verse is that some did not choose to receive their promises in this life, which is but a vapor and quickly passes away. They chose instead to keep their treasures for eternal life. Do we want to consume our rewards now or save them for eternity? When we really start to believe in the resurrection, *in our hearts and not just our minds*, we will be far more devoted to the eternal rather than the temporal. When we start caring more about souls than finances, the Lord will be able to trust us with more finances.

In Philippians 3:10-11, the Apostle Paul prayed to be conformed to the image of the Lord's death in order that he might attain to the resurrection. Paul's prayer was answered; he died alone, with most of his followers having scattered from him—just as the Lord had died.

Paul's last thoughts on earth may well have been to wonder if he had really accomplished anything through all his pain and sacrifice. He probably had no idea that the letters he had scribbled from prison even still existed, let alone that they would go on to become some of the most influential words ever written. It is probable that Paul is still reaping more fruit for eternal life through his letters than all of the present-day apostles combined! His words were eternal because his heart was focused on eternity.

Paul's ministry continues to bear fruit because he spoke the Word of God. Is that not the basic issue of ministry? It does not matter how many books we sell, how many people attend our meetings, or how many people we influence. The issue is this: Are we ministering the eternal Word of God?

9. The ability to receive correction is essential to walking in truth.

Proverbs contains some important directives for those who would seek the truth of Scripture.

Reproofs for discipline are *the* way of life (6:23).

Reprove a wise man, and he will love you (9:8).

**He is on the path of life who heeds instruction,
But he who forsakes reproof goes astray (10:17).**

**He whose ear listens to the life-giving reproof
Will dwell among the wise (15:31).**

**Cease listening, my son, to discipline,
And you will stray from the words of knowledge (19:27).**

The ability to receive correction is one of the most infallible signs of spiritual maturity and true spiritual authority. The mature have learned that the Lord disciplines those whom He loves. His discipline is essential if we are to remain on the path of life. Those who have received their authority from above will not be threatened by correction. The mature will be quick to admit their mistakes, regardless of how they may appear to others. They recognize that any true authority they have is established and maintained by God and is not subject to what people think.

10. Inflexibility destroys the ability to receive truth.

New wine cannot be put into an old wineskin (see Matthew 9:17). Wineskins are made of leather and can become brittle and rigid with age. Because new wine is in a state of expansion, it will cause an old wineskin to burst. New wine needs to be put into a new wineskin that is flexible and expandable.

People are the same way. When we become inflexible, we cannot receive spiritual truth. Truth is always living and expanding. No single human being has completely understood the depths of even the most simple biblical truths. When biblical truths stop expanding for us, they also cease to give us life. We must be on a continual journey of sinking our roots deeper into the Word of God.

As stated previously, the bride of Christ is to be **"without spot or wrinkle" (Ephesians 5:27).** The spots speak of sin;

the wrinkles speak of age. The true church is to remain perpetually youthful; she is not to acquire the wrinkles that inevitably come with human aging. The main quality which distinguishes youth from aging is growth. When we stop growing spiritually, we have begun the process of death, a process which could keep us from being a part of the bride that Jesus is returning for.

Recently, as I was walking and praying about what we could do to help children's ministries, the Lord hit me with one of those take-your-breath-away insights. He gently informed me that He did not want us to try and make the children "mature" Christians. He wanted the children to help make the "mature" Christians more like them! The kind of children's ministry that the Lord showed me was not so much a ministry *to* the children as it was *releasing children into ministry*. If we want to enter the kingdom, we must become like the children—not make them like us. We have more to learn from them than they do from us!

11. To keep from being deceived, we must be freed from the fear of deception.

Someone once said that fear is faith for the things you do not want. Over a period of time I've observed that my children had to *learn* fear—it was not natural to them. There is only one biblically sanctioned fear, which is the pure and holy fear of the Lord. If we have the right fear of the Lord, there is nothing else in this world that we should fear. Many walk in spiritual darkness even though they spend hours a day reading the Bible, simply because they have more faith in the enemy's power to deceive them than they have in the Lord's power to guide them into all truth.

In the Bible, "sheep" are often used as a metaphor for men because their characteristics are similar. Sheep are timid animals that are quickly overcome by the bondage to the familiar. They are very resistant to environmental changes. People are the same way. Even new converts can become "old wineskins" in a matter of months, becoming too rigid and inflexible to receive new truth.

Left to themselves, sheep will stay in the same pasture until they have utterly destroyed it by eating the grass right down to the roots. Often they would rather eat the nubs of grass in a known field than enter an unknown fresh, lush pasture. Are we not just like that at times? We preach the same truth and sing the same songs until we have squeezed every last drop of anointing out of them. Then we fear and reject those who are not just like us, but who have fresh food for our souls. We become weak from spiritual starvation before we will consider moving on to a new place or having any interchange with believers who may believe a little differently than we do. Bondage to the familiar has destroyed many.

A good shepherd will lead his flock to a new pasture before the one they are in is overly worked and the anointing destroyed. This allows for a return to the same pasture in the future. We too must learn to leave our spiritual feeding places while they are still fresh, allowing us to return to them for fresh food when it is needed. If we stay too long on the same emphasis, we will wear it out. Then we can never return to it.

If the genetic line of sheep is to stay healthy, they must occasionally crossbreed with other flocks. Every spiritual movement that has turned inward and ceased to interchange with other Christian groups has inevitably lost its life, power and vision. Isolated groups have inevitably drifted into extremes and serious error.

One of the most deadly enemies of truth is the spirit of territorial preservation. Sooner or later it will test the nature of every church leader. This spirit opens the door for the control spirit, which breeds inflexibility. This cuts off the believer's ability to receive the fresh, living waters from the Lord, which results in spiritual stagnation or death.

Another reason why flexibility and change are important is found in Jeremiah 48:11-12:

> **Moab has been at ease since his youth;**
> **He has also been undisturbed on his lees,**
> **Neither has he been emptied from vessel to vessel,**
> **Nor has he gone into exile.**
> **Therefore he retains his flavor,**
> **And his aroma has not changed.**
>
> **"Therefore behold, the days are coming," declares the LORD, "when I shall send to him those who tip vessels, and they will tip him over, and they will empty his vessels and shatter his jars" (Jeremiah 48:11-12).**

In Bible times, wine was purified by letting it sit in a vessel until the dregs had settled to the bottom. Then it was poured into a new vessel and allowed to sit so that the remaining impurities would settle. This was repeated until all the impurities were removed from the wine. The Lord contended that Moab had never been emptied into a new vessel; it maintained its dregs and was not pure. It is the changes in our lives which help to free us of the bondage to the familiar and keep us dependent on the Lord instead of on our environments.

Our spiritual life is purified in this same manner. The Lord allows us to remain in one place until the dregs in our life settle. Then He pours us into a new vessel—a new situation or environment. This new situation could be a different emphasis in the teaching He is giving us. He may move us to a different congregation or give our congregation new leadership, thus giving us a new job or a new supervisor. Change is crucial to maintaining purity in our lives. We are called to be spiritual sojourners, not squatters.

This is not to promote change just for the sake of change. The church has had a tendency to take every truth to the extreme before finding its proper balance. The answer to being overly restricted to one pasture is not to become a church hopper, or like the men of Athens who were only interested in hearing something new. If changes occur prematurely, the dregs do not have time to settle and nothing is accomplished. We need to stay with a certain emphasis until the truth is firmly rooted in us. Then we must be ready to embrace changes the Lord sends, understanding how essential these new truths are for our maturity.

Rightly Dividing the Word

There are many doctrinal and hermeneutical positions which actually promote a rigidity and inflexibility which destroy true Christian maturity. These breed the same pharisaical spirit which persecuted the Lord. Such positions are drawn from isolated scriptures such as **"There is nothing new under the sun" (Ecclesiastes 1:9),** which is taken to mean there is no further understanding to be had. This can be true in some areas, but terribly false and deceptive when used as a general truth.

How many totally new things has the Lord done just since that Scripture was first written? How about the other Scriptures which declare that He will **"do a new thing" (Isaiah 43:19 KJV), "declare new things" (Isaiah 42:9),** and create **"the new heavens and the new earth" (Isaiah 66:22)?**

To be properly understood, the Word of truth must be "rightly divided" (see II Timothy 2:15 KJV). Isolated scriptures, taken out of context, can be deceptive and destructive. Some passages of Scripture are an articulation of the human spirit, which the Lord included as part of the understanding we need. Because of this, every individual verse of Scripture is not God's Word in the sense that it is a statement from Him of His perfect will.

There are statements in the Bible that are actually made by Satan. Just because something is stated in the Bible does not mean it is automatically "God's Word," or position. Some things are included in Scripture so that we can better understand Satan's schemes, not for us to use them for establishing doctrine.

Scripture also records statements made by men in their bitterness or rebellion. These are not God's position either. For instance, a psalmist wrote that those who smashed the Babylonian babies against the rocks would be blessed. Taken out of context, it could be concluded from this Scripture that the Lord will bless those who smash the babies of their enemies. To the contrary, Jesus commanded us to *love* our enemies.

There is important revelation in the book of Ecclesiastes, but for this revelation to be properly applied one must understand that this book is written from a position of being **"under the sun,"** or from the earthly perspective. From this perspective everything does seem to be vanity of vanities—without meaning or purpose.

There are statements in Ecclesiastes which are purposely contrary to other statements in the Bible. They are meant to show how our perspective is distorted when we see only from an earthly position. How many of those who preach that there is nothing new under the sun also preach that the spirit of man and beast is the same, that man is a beast, and that one has no advantage over the other as they all go to the same place when they die? This is stated in Ecclesiastes 3:18-22.

Some translators have added the word "like" before animals, obviously unable to comprehend why Scripture would state that men "are" animals. In these translations, "like" is usually italicized since it is not found in the original manuscripts. From the earthly perspective, men and animals are the same. This is a central point of Ecclesiastes, but it is not God's position.

The Ultimate Delusion

Those who say that they have the full revelation of God's truth are obviously in serious delusion. They might be compared to the aborigine who says he knows all there is to know about astrophysics. We have not yet fathomed the depths of the riches of wisdom and knowledge about even the simplest spiritual truths. How many have even begun to grasp the significance of such truths as the Melchizedek priesthood mentioned in the epistle to the Hebrews? Yet, the writer of this book, after expounding on such subjects, stated that he was only speaking about things which are as spiritual milk for spiritual babies!

If Hebrews was to be but milk for the early church, where does that place the learned twentieth- century church? We are presumably still in the womb, having learned much over the centuries but understanding little. Until the preconceptions and false doctrines which quickly turn us into old wineskins are cast off, they will continue to prevent a true church from true spiritual maturity.

If we could swallow our pride long enough to see ourselves in the light of biblical testimony, we would be shocked. Even the most spiritual and powerful churches in existence today are far from the spiritual stature and maturity of the most immature and unspiritual churches of the first century. The first-century church did not even have the compiled Bible and lacked the books, tapes, television programs and a host of other aids we take for granted. Books and teaching materials can be helpful—but are we in danger of learning much, yet somehow not coming to the knowledge of the truth? For the honest seeker of truth and the Divine will, nothing so stifles spiritual maturity as much as the tendency to resist change.

Conservatism has its place in maintaining order and a proper environment for growth, but not when it encourages debilitating shackles which prohibit the necessary advancement of the church. Valid conservatism is marked by stability and maturity. When the wine of God's truth expands, mature and stable leaders are needed to keep the church from being blown about by every new wind of doctrine. As Peter related in his second epistle, the unstable and untaught will distort the Scriptures (II Peter 3:16). There are those who will carry every truth to extremes. We cannot allow immature extremists to affect the church's searching for and growing in truth, either by receiving the extremes, or by overreacting to them.

When we talk about the wine of God's truth expanding or about receiving new revelation, we are not talking about adding to either the canon of Scripture or to the truths held by the first-century church. The modern revelations of God's truth, which have resulted in the increasing life and maturity of the advancing church, are all merely restorations of the truths held by the early church that were lost during the Dark Ages.

Each successive generation has had the tendency to feel that all such truth had already been recovered. However, the Holy Spirit has continued to give enlightenment which proves the contrary. Each time we recover a truth through the enlightenment of the Holy Spirit, we wonder how we could have missed anything so obvious in the Scriptures. What was unseen by the brightest or the most spiritual now becomes clear. How many more truths are yet to be restored? How many truths are not yet seen because the enlightenment has not yet been given? This we cannot presume to know without a debilitating spiritual arrogance that itself keeps us from the truth.

12. We must maintain our first love if we are to walk in truth.

Although God's truth continues to expand, the canon of Scripture is complete. This is verified by the Scripture itself. The Bible is a complete story as it is; it has a conclusion. Who has comprehended the depth in even the most elementary books of the Bible? How could we need more than what is written there?

To think that we have all of the truth is prideful. God resists the proud, and He may have to go around us to find others who can contain His new wine. **"The Spirit searches all things, even the depths of God" (I Corinthians 2:10).** As we read the Bible with the guidance of the Holy Spirit, we will see more each time we read it. Though there is nothing new under the sun, there is plenty that is new to us!

The Word of God is a river, not a pond! It is flowing, moving, going somewhere. In Ephesians 5:26, the Word is compared to water because they have similar characteristics. Both must keep flowing in order to stay pure. When God's Word stops flowing through us, it will settle into puddles and become stagnant very quickly.

Openness to new and fresh insights into the Word does not mean that we become careless with what we receive. We are called to maintain the spiritual nobility of the Bereans, who carefully examined the Scriptures to verify the new things that they were hearing (Acts 17:10-11). We are not seeking new things, but sound scriptural TRUTH. We must remain tolerant and open, but also wise.

As we have discussed, *the first privilege lost by the fall was fellowship with God.* This fellowship is the primary goal of restoration, including the restoration of truth. Restoration of fellowship is the purpose of redemption and should be the first and main goal in the life of every soul redeemed. Our fellowship with God is the first priority of true Christianity and the primary issue that distinguishes Christianity from all other religions.

True Christianity is the restoration of union with God. The restoration of man's fellowship with God permeates the entire Bible. If we seek truth for any other reason, it can distort what we receive. The quality of the understanding we are receiving can be measured directly by how much closer it draws us to the Lord. The issue of truth is not how much we know about God—it is how well we are abiding in Him.

One of the greatest factors distorting the character and nature of Christianity is our tendency to forget this basic truth: Our first calling is to fellowship—not to works and not just to understanding. True understanding of the Bible is dependent on our union with the Author.

Chapter 21

THE WORD IS A SEED

In the parable of the sower, Jesus explained that **"the seed is the word of God" (Luke 8:11)**. The seed is not the plant, but it already contains the genetic code of what the plant will be. If we understand the nature of the seed in the Word, it will enable us to understand both the nature of the Word which has been planted in us and what it will be when it matures.

Just as a natural seed contains the genetic code of the mature plant, the spiritual seed initially planted in a person's life to produce faith will be a determining factor in the quality of that person's spiritual life. That is why the Lord Jesus never compromised the conditions for following Him. He knew that the quality of the word a person first responded to would work to define the quality of that person's faith. When we lower the standards of initial commitment in order to fill our meetings or our evangelistic reports, we are also working to weaken the entire spiritual fabric of the church.

Another important characteristic of every seed is that it has a built-in mechanism to prevent it from sprouting until conditions are right for growth. The conditions required for growth are light, water and heat. The proper amounts of all three must be present. A combination of two out of the three of these will not cause the seed to open. This is to keep the seed from being fooled by an early warm spell that is wet when it is still winter. If there is not also enough light, it will not sprout. Nor will the seeds sprout during cold or dry spells in the spring, even though there is sufficient light. The Lord put this genius in the seeds because the seed is the foundation of all life.

This is also true about spiritual seeds. God has placed in them a mechanism which will prevent their sprouting until the conditions are right for growth. The same three characteristics are required in their proper amounts for the opening of spiritual seeds: water, heat and light. Water speaks of the Word of God. Light speaks of the revelation which gives illumination to the Word. Heat speaks of the right circumstances.

Until all the conditions are properly met, the spiritual seed will not sprout either. We can force a decision out of the person when the conditions are not right, but his life will not really change, except perhaps on a superficial level to comply with the pressure we have applied.

A person must be born again to see the kingdom of God. The seed, the Word of God, must sprout in that person if the conversion is to be real. That is why Jesus called only a very few people to immediate commitment. He only called those to an immediate commitment who He discerned were ready. The majority of His ministry was devoted to sowing seeds for future reaping by the church.

In I Corinthians 3:6, the apostle Paul recounted how he had planted, Apollos had watered and God had caused the harvest. If our ministry is to be effective, we need this same discernment. We must know when it is time to plant and when it is time to reap, or when to just water seeds that have already been planted, trusting God to send someone else to reap at the proper time.

There has been a very prevalent "reaping mentality" in evangelism which has often been detrimental to the true work of evangelism. We only seem to count those who "make a decision," regardless of whether the conversions are real or not. By far the majority of conversions at evangelistic meetings have proven not to be real. Yet an evangelist who just sows seeds and has no "head count" to put in his report will seldom continue to receive the support he needs. By working this way, we are forgetting an important scriptural principle. Those who reap only have something to reap because someone else was faithful to plant the seeds.

Evangelism is actually a *process*: sowing the seed, allowing God to provide it with proper water, heat and light, then reaping at the proper time.

The Nature of Truth

The nature of truth is found in Ecclesiastes 3:1-8: **"There is an appointed time for everything. And there is a time for every event under heaven—a time to give birth, and a time to die; a time to plant, and a time to uproot [reap] what is planted."** Reaping is a truth, and it is an important part of the ministry, but if we are trying to reap when it is time to sow, we have been deceived. Deception is not being in God's will. If we are not in His will, we will not have the proper timing.

The same is true in the ministry of teaching. There is a time to plant seeds, a time to water them, and a time to reap. We cannot always expect an immediate result from our teaching. We can only be faithful to plant, water or reap as we are directed by the Lord. He must watch over His seeds and bring forth a harvest at the proper time.

A large amount of the frustration felt by pastors is caused by their failure to understand this. The frustration many congregations have with their pastors is due to the same. When the pastor or teacher pressures the congregation to bring forth fruit prematurely, the result will be artificial fruit. Have you ever tried to bite an artificial apple? That is how much of the church's fruit tastes to the world and to the Lord!

The Seed Must Be Tested

The Lord explained in the parable of the sower that every word of God would be tested in three basic ways before it could bear fruit. Understanding this parable will help us to bear more true spiritual fruit from the truths we receive.

Test Number One: The birds of the air. In giving His interpretation of this parable the Lord referred to the birds as Satan. **"When anyone hears the word of the kingdom, *and does not understand it*, the evil one comes and snatches away what has been sown in his heart" (Matthew 13:19).** Having a personal understanding of truth is essential if we are to bear the fruit of the Word. When people are pressured into trying to produce, the result will not be the true fruit of the Spirit.

There was a point in the Lord's ministry when He asked His disciples who men said that He was. They answered that some said He was a prophet, some thought He was Elijah, and some considered Him to be a resurrected John the Baptist. Then He challenged them with *"Who do YOU say that I am?"* **(Matthew 16:15)** If they were to be His disciples, they could not just parrot what other men said about Him. They had to know Him for themselves.

This is still true. It does not matter who our pastor, our favorite teacher, author or televangelist says Jesus is. We must each have our own revelation from the Father of who He is. No one will attain salvation or grace by another man's faith. We cannot be converted to another man's Jesus; He must be our *own* Jesus. We must each have our *own* revelation of Him and of every truth that He gives us to bear fruit with. Otherwise we remain easy prey for the birds of the air, who will surely come to steal our seed.

Let those who are in leadership be especially wary of this test. Without a continuing personal commitment to Jesus, there is no true fruit in our ministry. We cannot be satisfied merely with the "amens" of those whom we serve. When the testing comes, there will be nothing left of our work *if* those we serve follow us without having their own understanding of the Word.

Those who teach should always promote the noble spirit of the Bereans, who searched the Scriptures for themselves when they heard the message in order to verify its truth. The leader who seeks blind faith from his followers will only have blind followers. True faith is not blind; it is the very essence of illumination and understanding.

Those who **"do not understand the word"** will have it stolen. Those with true spiritual authority do not fear challenges from their people—they appreciate them, knowing that they are evidence that the word is being taken seriously. The only ones who never question the teachings they receive are those who do not really care.

Again, true Christianity does not consist of just being able to expound truth accurately, or even behaving properly according to the biblical exhortations. True Christianity is nothing less than union with Christ. This union is not found in our minds, but in our hearts. It is **"Christ *in you*, the hope** of glory" (Colossians 1:27). It is only when truth has reached our heart that it will it be our life. It is not the one who has truth in these days who will be kept from deception, but the one who has **"the *love* of the truth" (II Thessalonians 2:10).** We will only have a love for the truth when it has reached our hearts.

Test Number Two: Shallowness is the next great test of the seed. Some received the word with great joy, but as soon as hardship or persecution arose because of the word, they quickly abandoned what they had just received.

One of the banes of modern Christianity has been our tendency to esteem most highly those who grow the fastest. These are often the very works the Lord warned us about in this parable. Some seeds sprout quickly because they have little root or depth. Largeness and fast growth are not necessarily signs of God's approval. The works which will endure are not necessarily those which have been quick to extend their branches, but those which have been diligent to sink their roots deep. If the foundation is weak, it does not matter how strong the rest of the building is; it is in danger of collapse. The bigger the building, the greater the danger because of the increased pressure upon the foundation.

We are called to be **"oaks of righteousness" (Isaiah 61:3).** This is a very appropriate metaphor, because it accurately relates to a characteristic God desires to form in us. A healthy oak tree will have a root system at least as extensive as its branches. Like the oak tree, we should never extend our branches (our outreaches) beyond the limits of our root system. If we do, like the oak we will be in danger of toppling during a storm or strong wind.

There is another characteristic of the oak tree which is relevant to the believer. An oak actually becomes stronger during dry spells. On a normal summer day a mature oak tree will release about forty gallons of water into the atmosphere through a process called "transpiration." During droughts, it stops this release of water to channel it back to the roots so they can grow deeper and find the deeper waters.

We must stop bemoaning the dry or hard times; they work for our good. Like the oak tree, we must use them as encouragement to find deeper waters. God has given each of us a well of living waters which will never run dry. We will never be dry if we learn how to go to the well.

Jesus said, **"He who believes in Me, as the Scripture said, 'From his innermost being shall flow rivers of living water'" (John 7:38).** When we get dry, it is because we are abiding in a place that is too shallow. All of the dry times are meant to help us find the source that never runs out.

Test Number Three: The cares and worries of the world. God's unshakeable kingdom **"is not of this world" (John 18:36).** If our attention is upon this world, we cannot see His kingdom. If we are in Christ, we are supposed to have died to this world. If we are dead to the world, what can the world possibly do to us? It is impossible for a dead man to fear, to be offended, or to feel rejection. It is impossible for a dead man to desire or lust after the things of the world, and thus become overly concerned about gaining or losing them.

In Luke 14:33, the Lord Jesus Himself plainly stated, **"No one of you can be My disciple who does not give up** *all* **his own possessions."** Does this mean that we must sell everything we own in order to follow Him? Not necessarily. This was not literally required of all who followed Him when He was on earth, so we should not conclude that it will be required of all of us in a literal way today. But it was literally required of some then, and it will be required of some who follow Him today. We do know that, whether it is literal or spiritual, "all" of our possessions will be affected.

The Lord clearly said **"no one"** could be His disciple without giving up **"all his own possessions."** For some, this may be literal as it was with the rich young ruler. For others, it may involve a radical separation from our devotion to our possessions so that they have no pull on us, whether we gain them or lose them. Separation from things must be accomplished if we are to be true disciples, for where our treasure is, there will our heart be also (Matthew 6:21). It is by the heart that we believe. As the apostle Paul warned us in his letter to Timothy:

> **But godliness actually is a means of great gain, when accompanied by contentment.**
>
> **For we have brought nothing into the world, so we cannot take anything out of it either.**

And if we have food and covering, with these we shall be content.

But those who want to get rich fall into temptation and a snare and many foolish and harmful desires which plunge men into ruin and destruction.

For the love of money is a root of all sorts of evil, and some by longing for it have wandered away from the faith, and pierced themselves with many a pang.

But *flee from these things,* you man of God; and pursue righteousness, godliness, faith, love, perseverence and gentleness.

Fight the good fight of faith, take hold of eternal life (I Timothy 6:6-12).

Bondage to the material reveals that we believe only in our minds and not in our hearts. When we believe in our hearts, eternal things become more real than temporary things. The temporary can no longer keep us yoked to them. When our treasure really is in heaven, our hearts will be there also.

But not all the cares and worries of this world are related to material possessions. Some are based on the choking bondage to men's approval. This is also the prevailing of the temporary over the eternal. Jesus asked, **"How can you believe when you receive glory from one another, and do not seek the glory that is from the one and only God?"** (John 5:44) Seeking honor or recognition from men, even spiritual men, instead of maintaining the **"simplicity and purity of**

devotion to Christ" (II Corinthians 11:3) is a grievous enemy of true faith.

Developing a secret relationship with our Father in heaven is one of the more positive things we can do to grow in faith. The Lord exhorted us to give alms and to pray in secret. If we do things to receive recognition from men, then we have received our whole reward by getting that temporary, fleeting recognition. If we do things only before the Father, then our treasure in heaven grows. **"Where your treasure is there will your heart be also" (Matthew 6:21).** As our treasure in heaven grows, so will our attention increase upon the things that are eternal instead of being so consumed by all that is to pass away.

Our basic lack of faith can often be traced to our care and concern for the things of the world. This is not only undesirable, it is not tolerable for a true disciple of Christ. If our treasure is in heaven with Christ, our hearts will be there with Him. Then our hearts will be fertile ground to bring forth the fruit of true faith: some thirty, some sixty and some one hundred fold. The Lord said that if we had faith as small as a mustard seed that we could move mountains. The seed may be the smallest thing that we have, but it can yield awesome results when given to God.

Elijah required that the widow give him all the meal and oil that she had, which was hardly enough for a single meal. When she gave it to him, she never ran out. Had she withheld the tiny bit that she had, she would almost certainly have starved. Her little bit released to God became an endless supply. Our lives are just like that. Compared to eternity we are all but a vapor. Why not give it all to Him and see what He can do with it? By doing that, we will put ourselves in the place where we can touch eternity.

Chapter 22

Fundamentals
of Biblical
Interpretation

In this chapter we will examine the basics of proper biblical interpretation. We will also take a cursory look at the two most basic, but opposite, hermeneutical systems of biblical interpretation, along with the merits and stumbling blocks of each.

The first principle in proper biblical interpretation is to understand that Scripture is the final authority **"for teaching, for reproof, for correction, for training in righteousness; that the man of God may be adequate, equipped for every good work" (II Timothy 3:16-17).** Even our opinion of Scripture must be formed by what Scripture says about itself. A valid system of biblical interpretation will only use the principles that are used by the authors of Scripture in their references to other Bible passages.

To declare that the Bible is the final authority will sometimes bring the protest: "No, *Jesus* is the Head of the church and is therefore the final authority." But even Jesus Himself repeatedly appealed to the authority of Scripture as the basis for His actions and His teaching. When challenged by Satan or human adversaries, He might have replied, "I am the Son of God and I am doing things by My own authority." Instead He was always careful to state the basis for His position as being *"It is written."* If such was Jesus' devotion to Scripture, how much more should it be ours?

What Does the Bible Say?

Few genuine seekers of truth and understanding dispute that the Bible is the final authority for doctrine. "The Bible says" ends all questions, except what is called "the great question"—*What does the Bible really say?* Different schools of biblical interpretation are often in basic conflict with each other on this point.

The interpretation of any single passage can yield a multitude of differing opinions, even within the same schools of interpretation. We should recognize the differences between the two most extreme schools of interpretation in order to at least have a "grid" for understanding and evaluating most of the other methods and their conclusions.

Our primary goal in studying hermeneutics is for **"rightly dividing the word of truth" (II Timothy 2:15 KJV).** We seek to accurately determine what the Bible says so that we can live it and teach it. Our secondary goal is to give maturing saints, emerging ministries, and those holding leadership positions in the body of Christ an understanding of the source of many of the confusing teachings and destructive heresies they will inevitably face from time to time. Not understanding the sources of spurious teachings will limit our power to combat them.

As we evaluate these two opposite systems of interpretation, we must avoid the tendency to make overgeneralizations or judge others as "extreme" because they may use some of the precepts from what we classify as an extreme position. The great majority of teachers, ministers and believers stand somewhere in between these extremes in their approach to Scripture. Whether or not they know or admit it, most students of the Bible use some elements from each position, because there is merit to both sides, and both are used by those who wrote Scripture.

Our purpose in evaluating these approaches is to find and use that which is valuable and avoid the stumbling blocks. We must also understand that all who hold to the precepts of either of these extreme positions still do not draw the same conclusions about every passage of Scripture.

The Literal Method of Interpretation

The literal method of interpretation is the position held by most of the ultraconservative Evangelical schools. A distinction does need to be made between the ultraconservative camp and those who are merely conservative. Conservatives are committed to the inspiration and inerrancy of Scripture, but give more liberty to the different interpretations of it.

It should also be noted that many of the camps that are considered liberal by the ultraconservatives are really conservative. These are conservatives who believe in the inspiration and inerrancy of Scripture, and also use the literal method of interpretation as the basis for their exegesis. But these conservatives give liberty for the other methods of interpretation when it appears to be necessary for proper exegesis.

The true liberal camp does not believe in the inerrancy or inspiration of Scriptures. This is why I am here using the term *ultra*conservatives. I want to give a place to those who are truly conservative but do not fit into the more extreme categories.

The basic creed of the pure literal method is, *"Inspiration does not render redundant the necessity of interpretation, and no passage of Scripture discloses its meaning to us apart from actual exegesis."* This sounds safe and practical, and it *is* the safe and practical place to *begin* to understand the Bible. Nevertheless, it is clear that the Bible itself repeatedly violates this principle.

When some of the biblical authors interpret other passages of Scripture, they sometimes deviate from this rule.

The Allegorical Method of Interpretation

There are times when literal exegesis yields no intelligible interpretation because the passage is obviously meant to be allegorical. Although seemingly the opposite of the literal method, the allegorical method of interpretation is nevertheless important. For example, consider Galatians 4:21-31, where Paul explains that *"This is allegorically speaking:* **for these women [Sarah and Hagar] are two covenants" (verse 24).** This passage has been the greatest thorn to the ultraconservatives who have crusaded against allegorical or mystical interpretation of Scripture.

There are many other passages of Scripture which must be interpreted allegorically to make sense, such as when Jesus is referred to as **"the Lamb of God" (John 1:29).** Jesus' purpose in becoming a man cannot be fully understood apart from understanding His role as the "Lamb," but this title is obviously not intended to be literal. We could go on to mention the references to Jesus as "the high priest," as "a priest forever according to the order of Melchizedek," as being seated upon the "throne of David," and many other examples.

To be unyielding in using the literal method of interpretation generally results in something between confusion and the ridiculous. We would have to believe that Jesus is coming back to judge literal sheep and goats, or that grass is going to hell. The only escape is to allow for interpretation according to "what the writer of the passage meant." This is helpful, but still allows for a considerable diversity of opinion as to just what the writer did mean. It is clear that biblical writers themselves did not always know or understand what they were writing. This is especially true of Bible prophecies.

Chapter 23

The Universal Problem with Spiritual Principles

Spiritual principles do not cease to be useful just because they do not apply to every situation. We must guard against the tendency to swing to the some other extreme when problems arise with our basic principles. We tend to think of principles as always having to be consistent and without exception, but there is a difference between laws and principles. Principles can be expected to have some exceptions.

With the humility that is required if we are to come to the knowledge of the truth, we need to admit that even our most cherished principles may sometimes need to be modified or even changed. It can be argued that there are no absolute principles of biblical interpretation and that this is by the

Lord's design. He does not want His people to trust solely in principles for understanding. He wants us to depend on Him in order to come to the knowledge of the truth. Even so, this does not nullify a proper use of some principles, as long as we understand their limitations.

The church is relieved of a terrible legalistic burden when we realize that even the best and most consistent principles of biblical interpretation are limited. If we are to receive the truth, the Holy Spirit must lead us. There are principles that can help to keep us within the general region of the path that leads to life, but if we put our trust solely in our principles, no matter how biblically based they seem to be, we have already departed from the place where we can hear the Holy Spirit.

For the past few years, I have tried to read at least one or two books a year on hermeneutics. All of them give lip service to the need to be led by the Holy Spirit in our search for truth. Yet the systems they promote usually give no room for being led by Him. In fact, many of the principles taught in these books work to destroy a believer's ability to hear from the Lord in interpreting Scripture.

I have not read every book on hermeneutics, therefore I do not presume that this is true of all the books available. And even with this prevailing element in the books I read, I still benefited from them. To eat this meat we must watch for the bones—and there are some big ones to watch for!

Trying to Avoid Traps Can Create Bigger Ones

Some of those in the literal school have addressed the problem of dealing with obvious allegories in Scripture by establishing another principle: that only those who wrote Scripture have the authority to interpret its allegories. Even having this principle contradicts their own basic premise that Scripture is not allegorical but always literal. In addition, their premise of allowing only those with the authority to write Scripture the authority to interpret its allegories opens the door wide to another, even more dangerous assumption.

Daniel was told to conceal his words and seal up the book until the time of the end (Daniel 12:4). The parts of Daniel's revelation that were explained to him confirmed that what he had seen was allegorical. For instance **"the ram which you saw with the two horns *represents* the kings of Media and Persia" (Daniel 8:20)** and the four beasts **"are four kings who will arise from the earth" (Daniel 7:17).** If only those with the authority to write Scripture have the authority to interpret its allegories, who will explain all that has not yet been interpreted from Daniel? Mystery still shrouds most of the book. Further, who is going to interpret all the other prophetic books, such as the Book of Revelation, which contain many stated allegories?

The apostles did not interpret these for us. Did God give these allegories just to tease us? Certainly not! When someone produces the obvious interpretations, does that give them authority to write Scripture? Of course not! Many of the principles which have been developed to give safety to biblical interpretation open the door for even worse problems.

Some contradictions can easily be seen in every one of the principles of biblical interpretation. Many honest theologians acknowledge this. There seem to be exceptions to every rule, but that does not automatically invalidate those rules. Those who have discarded all the rules have fallen into some of the most destructive heresies of all. Seeking to be free of legalism, they have fallen into a general lawlessness regarding their interpretation of the Bible.

The role of *proper restraints* is similar to the role of tracks for a train. Both are restraints which keep something from wandering where it should not go. But without the restraints there would be no movement at all! The tracks that restrain the train also set it free to be what it was created to be and to operate with confidence and speed. Proper restraints on biblical interpretation set people free to explore the Scriptures and arrive at the Truth without fear of going off into destructive errors.

The literal method of interpretation is the basis for proper scriptural exegesis, and this is the method most used by the Bible to interpret itself. But literal interpretation was never meant to be an exclusive method. Extreme positions inevitably lead to contradictions and counterproductive overreactions. Many of these positions would not have been extreme if they had just been presented with some flexibility.

There are many outstanding principles of biblical interpretation that have been illuminated through the development of conservative evangelical hermeneutics. We need to take the good from this system while rejecting its destructive, reactionary elements.

The Danger from Reactionaries

The allegorical system of biblical interpretation is the extreme opposite of the literal system. Without question, much of the Bible is allegorical, so the allegorical method must be used at times to properly understand the Scriptures.

However, using the allegorical system as the foundational method of interpretation leads to the inclination to see more of the Scripture as allegorical than was intended. Seeing Scripture first from an allegorical perspective can dangerously dilute the important foundational doctrines of the faith. This system usually results in "free association," or the arbitrary interpretation of isolated references and passages to justify a predetermined position or doctrine.

The allegorical method of interpretation, when carried to its logical conclusion, has frequently resulted in destructive heresies. Even so, there is a problem in overreacting and throwing out the entire method. Totally discarding the system may save us from falling out of the boat on one side, while it throws us out of the boat on the other side. Overreactions to both extreme positions have led to the perversion of the Scriptures.

As stated, new wine requires new wineskins that are flexible and expandable. Despite the determination of its proponents to esteem and honor the Scriptures, ultraconservative evangelical hermeneutics can lead to a deadly and pervasive form of humanism. This humanism can actually replace God. Man, and the hermeneutical principles man has developed, then become the interpreter of Scripture. The result is a rigidity and a "knee jerk" paranoia which would stifle every new move of God, just as it sought to stifle the very moving of God Himself when He came to walk among us. **"For the letter kills, but the Spirit gives life" (II Corinthians 3:6).**

Those who fall into the extreme use of allegory usually succumb to a modern form of Gnosticism. They usually go on to believe that only the initiated few can understand the true, hidden meaning of the Scriptures. This usually releases one of the most deadly forms of pride.

Placing sole reliance upon hermeneutic principles of exegesis completely removes the seeker from the needed personal encounter with the Lord to receive truth. Those who rely only on principles no longer recognize the ability of the Holy Spirit to lead them to truth. Many conservative evangelical principles of hermeneutics have done nearly as much to remove the living word from believers as the Latin Mass did during the Middle Ages. This system makes the believer dependent upon "professionals," those who comprise a priestcraft of their own.

It is true that the church could have avoided some of the most destructive heresies had she complied with some of the hermeneutic principles of ultraconservatives. However, in doing this, she would also have probably missed nearly every visitation of the Lord. That is exactly what happened to the ultraconservatives' spiritual forefathers, the Pharisees. Many of the cures which have been contrived to protect the church from heresy have turned out to be worse than the disease they sought to eradicate.

Understanding Allegory

The allegorical method of biblical interpretation is basically an attempt to see the hidden or deeper meaning in the Scriptures. There are definitely some hidden meanings in the Scriptures, and some of the more obvious ones are found in the prophetic books such as Daniel and Revelation. The book of Hebrews explains how many of the Old Covenant rituals and experiences were models or "types" of their New Covenant fulfillment. The picture of Jesus as the "high priest" is just one example. Many of the other New Testament books are also seeded with examples of this, such as where Jesus is referred to as "our Passover" (I Corinthians 5:7) and the rock which followed Israel in the wilderness (I Corinthians 10:4). Other examples could be cited as well, such as the text we have already noted in Galatians 4.

Many Bible scholars have considered typology a separate method of interpretation, distinguished from the allegorical method. There is a case for doing this, but biblical types really are allegories. An approach which gives room for typology has often been used to accommodate the obvious allegorical examples in Scripture, while allowing for a continued rejection of the use of allegory. However, it can be argued that there is no real difference between allegory and typology.

Many who use the allegorical method of interpretation claim they are trying to be totally dependent on the Holy Spirit to give them the interpretation of Scripture. This is certainly a noble motive. The problem occurs in distinguishing what is taught by the Spirit and what actually has its source in the person's own mind, or worse, what is taught by an evil spirit.

The Lord Himself did say that His sheep would know His voice (see John 10:27). Being able to distinguish His voice is one of the most important elements in the true Christian walk. Tragically, mostly because of a lack of equipping, many Christians require years of experience before they get to the place where they can consistently distinguish the Lord's voice from the multitude of other voices around them. Yet, most Christians form their basic doctrines and disciplines for biblical interpretation near the beginning of their spiritual lives.

A teacher is not just someone who knows and uses the right principles of biblical interpretation. Neither is a teacher just someone who can expound doctrine accurately. A true teacher is someone who has become a vessel through whom *The Teacher* can manifest Himself to meet the needs of His church. Yet, we must ask, how many teachers who have had such influence in the formation of the doctrines of the modern church truly reflect the character or nature of Jesus the Teacher?

This is obviously why the Lord instituted the congregational leadership through elders. An elder is not just someone who is wise; he is someone who is *old.* The reason that age is emphasized for those who would be in church leadership is that age represents experience. Someone once said, "Only experience can keep one from making mistakes, but experience comes from making mistakes." The Lord did not say that His *lambs* would know His voice. He said the ones who would know His voice were His *sheep*—those who were fully developed and mature.

Of course, just being physically old does not guarantee either wisdom or experience. Some of the most destructive heresies in church history have come late in the lives of some who had previously lived very fruitful Christian lives. Even so, age and experience usually help to keep us on the right course and enable us to discern the voice of the Lord. The reason mature sheep know their shepherd's voice the best is because they have been with him longer.

Sure Foundations

Paul explained that **"it is required of stewards that one be found trustworthy" (I Corinthians 4:2).** The Lord has ordained that we should only receive those whose credibility has been established, who have been **"found trustworthy."** Jeremiah asked, **"Who has *stood* in the council of the LORD,** that he should see and hear His word?" (Jeremiah 23:18) This word "stood" reflects the requirement for both faithfulness to the Lord and longevity if we are to hear Him and see His Word.

When Jesus was asked by what authority He did His works, His reply was a question for His inquisitors: **"Was the Baptism of John from heaven, or from men?"** (Mark 11:30) This was not meant to deflect their question. The answer to His question was the answer to their question. Even though He was the Son of God and the very Creator of the universe, Jesus both possessed and referred to His human credentials. This was important because, as the Redeemer of man, He had to come as "the Son of man."

John the Baptist was the last member and representative of the old order—the Law and the Prophets. From the very beginning, those who walked with God foretold the coming of the Messiah. John was there to represent them all, to point to the One of Whom they were all speaking. In a sense, they had all prepared the Lord's way and had baptized the people in the expectation of Him. Jesus did not scorn John as being "the old order." He honored him and those he represented by being baptized by John. He then acknowledged that baptism as the authority by which He did His works.

The Lord's own life and actions comprise the most basic Christian doctrine. Should we not follow His example in submitting ourselves to those who have preceded us? If we do not immerse ourselves in the teaching and works of those who have gone before us, our spiritual authority will be limited, at best.

This does not imply that we have to totally accept every teaching and practice of the previous spiritual generations. John the Baptist was not perfect, and it is obvious that he did not fully understand the Lord. Even after he had baptized Jesus, he later asked if Jesus was indeed the One he was looking for. Nevertheless, God has ordained that we must first submit to those who have preceded us before we can go forward. This gives us roots, stability and a strong foundation upon which to safely build, so we can press ahead in pursuit of more revelation of the truth contained in the Scriptures.

We may look back at Martin Luther's teaching and view it as basic to the point of being archaic, and some of it is when measured by today's understanding. Some of it is also erroneous, and would even provide the Nazis with a theological basis for their persecution of the Jews. Yet, Luther stood as a great light against the terrible darkness of his day. What he accomplished with the light that he had has not been equaled since, and there has not arisen a greater prophetic voice in the history of the church.

Martin Luther may not have had as much scriptural understanding as those who came later, but he made the way for them to receive the greater light. Many others have done the same, making possible the depth of understanding that we have today. We should honor them in the ways that we can, just as the Lord honored John. As we perceive how they made the way, it also gives a continuity and clarity for the unfolding purposes of God. This imparts a greater confidence in where we stand and in where we are to go from here.

Chapter 24

A Great Weakness of the Modern Church

One of the significant and debilitating weaknesses in the contemporary church is our ignorance of history. There is a proverb which states, "Those who do not know history are doomed to repeat it." The truth of this proverb is well-established when we view it in the light of church history. Every spiritual generation has been inclined to make the same general mistakes as the previous one. This tragic cycle may not be broken until we are delivered from the arrogance which causes us to resist the teachings of those who have gone before us.

Understanding the old does not prohibit the receiving of the new thing God is doing. On the contrary, it gives us a stronger foundation for receiving the new without carrying it to extremes. When we receive new light, it needs to be viewed from the perspective of what we already know. Without this foundation, new revelation will be subject to the distortions of our own prejudices and personal weaknesses. This has been the bane of the allegorical system of biblical interpretation.

The most outlandish and destructive distortions of Scripture have come from those who are inclined to follow the allegorical method of interpretation. It may be hard to argue with the statement, "God showed me this," but we must do it when the circumstances require such a challenge.

Peter had been given **"the keys to the kingdom" (Matthew 16:19)** and was established as the undisputed leader of the church. However, when he did something new, such as taking the gospel to the Gentiles, even he was challenged by the elders of the church. His new teaching was tested by the other leaders until it was determined from the Scriptures and from the fruit that this course of action did indeed originate from God.

Paul took his revelation to Jerusalem for the same reason (see Galatians 2:1-2). If these two leaders needed to be so challenged, how much more should we challenge one another when we claim to have heard something new from the Lord? Those who walk in true spiritual authority are not intimidated by such challenges. Like Paul, they will walk a long way if they have to in order to find those of spiritual stature and maturity who can properly examine their doctrine. This is the biblical method for confirming doctrinal truth.

We must give one another the grace to hear directly from the Lord, and to hear something new, but we must not accept a new revelation until it has been thoroughly searched out in the light of the Scriptures. When the apostles searched out the matter of going to the Gentiles, many Scriptures and some of the Lord's own statements came to their remembrance. This helped to further establish the validity of Peter's actions and new revelation.

Peter went to the Gentiles because of a trance in which he saw a sheet lowered with ceremonially unclean animals, which he was told to **"kill and eat" (Acts 10:13)**. There could have been many interpretations for this, but when the Holy Spirit was given to the Gentiles, Peter had a direct confirmation of the validity of his interpretation. This not only gave him more confidence in his interpretation, it also gave him more confidence for his subsequent actions. After the council had searched out the whole matter in relation to the Scriptures, there was surety. The result was the greatest strategic change of course in the history of the church—the Gentiles would have the gospel preached to them and the age of the Gentiles began.

Peter was obviously right to take the actions of going to the Gentiles before he had assurance for this course. The church has almost always entered a new place and walked in a new direction before complete understanding has been given. That is at least partially what it means to **"walk by faith" (II Corinthians 5:7)**. But before something fresh is promulgated as a new teaching to the whole church, there should be fruit that can be judged (e.g., the Gentiles received the Holy Spirit) and confirmation from the Scriptures.

The Scriptures used for confirmation will often be ambiguous and unclear before our experience, but the experience should make their meaning clear. When the Scriptures become clear in their confirmation, the truth can be confidently established as doctrine.

The whole spiritual process of the Reformation has been one of increasing light and biblical understanding. All of this increasing light and understanding is but the recovery of truth that was lost by the church during the Dark Ages. Even the most cursory study of church history reveals a systematic pattern in which truth and understanding were removed from the church for a period that lasted about 1,200 years.

About 600 years ago, a systematic pattern for the restoration of that lost truth began and obviously continues. It is presumptuous, and potentially disastrous, for us to think that we now have *all* the revelation that must be restored to the church. It is safe to say that any "new" truth is going to be just a restoration of an "old" truth that can be biblically established, even though we may not see the "new" truth revealed in Scripture until after its restoration.

The main problem with the allegorical method of interpretation is that it can be so subjective in nature. It is easily diluted, distorted and confused by the individual's own prejudices, doctrines, insecurities, rebellion, bitterness and so on. If revelation is defined as a direct enlightenment from the Lord, then it can and should stand the test of a biblical challenge from other leaders and from the Scriptures. This will help to illuminate and separate any other influences and the tendency toward "free association."

Free association results in establishing the meaning of a biblical allegory without a clear linkage to other biblical precedents. Many destructive heresies have originated in this way. Even so, this is what Paul did when he declared that "the two women are two covenants." How could anyone reading the story of Sarah and Hagar ever come to the conclusion that these women represented the Old and New Covenants? Could this revelation have come by any form of hermeneutics or system of exegesis?

If the story of these two women has such a significant meaning, is it not right for us to expect that there are similar biblical stories that are loaded with teaching that illuminates the purposes of God? Only those of the most shallow spiritual understanding and insight can read the books of Ruth, Esther, the Song of Solomon and others without seeing the profound and powerful teachings they represent as allegories. The writer of the book of Hebrews boldly points back to the story of Abraham and Isaac as a **"type" (Hebrews 11:19).** He also declared that the Outer Tabernacle was likewise a **"symbol" (Hebrews 9:8-9).** Time and space prohibit a comprehensive listing of the many other biblical examples.

It is not possible to understand the Scriptures in the light that the apostles and writers of the New Testament did without understanding the biblical allegories. Yet none of them used allegories to establish doctrines, but only to illuminate them. This is the point at which many who lean toward the allegorical system of interpretation begin to depart from biblical truth.

It cannot be disputed that the Lord uses both the literal and the allegorical to teach us through His Word. We will not come to a proper understanding of the Bible without the ability to see both of them in their *proper* perspective. This will only be realized when we have learned to balance the judgment of the Scriptures and the leading of the Spirit.

Chapter 25

WHEN THE NEW TESTAMENT BECOMES ANOTHER LAW

The Bible is a most awesome and wonderful gift. Because it is such a wonderful gift, it is easy to make it into an idol, allowing it to take the place of a living relationship with the Lord. The Bible was never intended to take the place of the Lord Himself, or the Spirit Whom He sent to lead us into all truth.

Ironically, one of the most presumptuous examples of "free association" has been made by those of the ultraconservative, literal school in their interpretation of I Corinthians 13:10: **"But when the perfect comes, the partial will be done away."** They argue that **"the perfect"** referred to in this text is the Bible. This is claimed in spite of the fact that there is absolutely no biblical support for this interpretation, and there are many Scriptures that clearly contradict it.

This doctrine is used to justify the dispensationalist view that the gifts of the Spirit have been done away with because we now have the Bible. Yet this prediction of a day when the partial will be taken away does not just talk about the gift of prophecy and other manifestations of the Spirit, it includes **"knowledge"** as well. If the perfect has truly come, then knowledge must have been done away with also. Has knowledge been done away with yet? Such obvious distortions of Scripture are much easier to make when we want to justify a position or belief badly enough.

During the Reformation, the cry *sola scriptura* ("Scripture alone") arose from the Protestants as a protest against the Roman Catholic practice of esteeming the word of the pope above the authority of Scripture. In recent times, ultraconservatives have used this same cry to protest against the acceptance of the revelatory gift of prophecy in the church. They compare the use of the words "thus saith the Lord" to the papal claim of having authority over Scripture. While there certainly is abundant evidence of the abuse of those precious words "thus saith the Lord," the overreaction of the ultraconservatives has also caused a disregard for the truth and the integrity of the Scriptures. Overreaction leads to distortion and even the promotion of deception.

When we have an agenda that we are trying to validate or defend, there is a great danger that we will distort the meaning of Scripture, even violating our other basic beliefs to do it. If we read the Scriptures with a truly humble heart, we will not do so in an attempt to *justify* our positions, but rather we will be seeking *corrections* for our positions. We must let the Scriptures say what they say, and not try to make them say what we want them to say.

Most of us have been taught to think of the Old Testament as the Law and the New Testament as Grace. However, this is not necessarily true. The Old Covenant is the Letter, the New Covenant is the Spirit. If we read the New Testament with an Old Covenant heart, it will only be law to us. We will still have a dead religion in which righteousness is based on compliance with the written commandments rather than on a living relationship with our God. Likewise, if we read the Old Testament with a New Covenant heart, it will be living truth to us.

The Bible is a means, not an end. Our goal is not just to know the book of the Lord, but to know the Lord of the book. The many errors and divisions within the body of Christ are not due to faults in the Bible. The errors and divisions have come from our use of it. Some of the laws and principles that we have wrested from the New Testament rival the legalism advocated by the Pharisees! This has often caused us to measure our maturity and spirituality by how well we conform to the letter, rather than how well we are becoming conformed to the image of the Son. True spiritual maturity only comes from the forming of Jesus within us.

The fact that Jesus came to fulfill the Law did not mean He was limited only to actions that were listed in the Law. In fact, He set many new precedents. He was careful to take His stand on what was written. However, when asked by what authority He did His works, He pointed to something that had been an entirely new precedent in Israel—John's baptism.

The Lord went on to establish many other new precedents: the church, the offices of apostle, evangelist and pastor, and much more. The apostles themselves were given the freedom to implement new procedures for worship and church authority, as well as the freedom to reorder their lifestyles, which they did.

Compliance with the Bible does not mean doing only what is specifically "written." Those devoted to complying with the biblical testimony *can do* what does not conflict with Scripture. The Bible is meant to be a general guideline to keep us within the bounds of spiritual safety and fruitfulness. It is not meant to be another Law.

Many use the judgment "that is not scriptural" to condemn things which they personally do not agree with or understand. Such judgment is in conflict with New Covenant grace, especially when we use it to denounce actions which do not contradict the clear instruction of the New Testament. If those prone to use this standard to condemn others were examined by it themselves, they too would be found guilty in many things.

Some of the most widespread traditions in the church have no example in Scripture. These include church buildings, Sunday schools, most of the popular forms of church government such denominations and networks of churches, many of our forms of worship, extra-local fellowships, "medical" missionaries, missionary societies, many popular forms of spiritual warfare, and much more! Teaching tapes, books, videos, bookstores, nurseries and many other common resources today are not found in Scripture either. But it is erroneous to say that because they are not found in Bible they are therefore "not scriptural," as if they are in violation of God's will.

Of course, there are some who advocate doing away with everything that is not specifically authorized in Scripture. There is a strong case for a return to biblical simplicity, but not because present-day practices in the church are "unscriptural." This will only lead to a more rigid form of legalism. *There is liberty to do what is not specifically addressed in the Bible as long as our actions do not contradict what is written.*

If someone feels led to do something new, we must give them the liberty to do it. Then we have not only the right, but the responsibility, to judge it by its fruit. **"Grace and truth were realized through Jesus Christ" (John 1:17).** Grace is the freedom to try, and truth is the realization that the fruit of what we try will be, and should be, tested.

Let's take the issue of church government. This is an important issue because it relates to the very lordship of Jesus in His church. But if the Lord wanted utter compliance with the many details wrested from the Bible by those who promulgate their "New Testament patterns for the church," He could have been far more specific in His Word. The "New Testament patterns" for the church that I have studied all differ from one another, often on basic issues. The Scriptures are not as clear or specific as we so often try to make them. What we try to implement in this way, even in order to bring unity and fruitfulness to the church, only brings division.

The church is not the pattern for the church—*Jesus* is the pattern for the church. He is the One that we are to grow up into, not just an external form or procedure for church life. To devote too much attention to external forms will divert attention from what promotes the formation of Jesus within.

A return to the biblical example of simplicity in church government would result in a great release of power and fruitfulness in the church, but this cannot be implemented as a law. The only valid implementation of church government comes when Jesus is lifted up and all crowns are cast at His feet. True church government comes from the acknowledgment of Jesus as King in our midst. Then we will not be so inclined to again be **"led astray from the simplicity and purity of devotion to Christ" (II Corinthians 11:3)** to a wrong form of church government.

The best form of church government will still be bad government if we do not have the right people in it. It is true that the wrong form of government can limit the effectiveness of even the right people, but the foundation of true spiritual authority is found in the Lord's authority in and through people, not in a system. When the right people walk in true spiritual authority, they will have the necessary wisdom to implement the best form of government. Until we have the new wine, we do not need a new wineskin. The new wine will give definition to the new wineskin it requires, but it is not the other way around.

Even though we do not want to be in error at all, if we are going to err, it is better and safer to err on the side of grace. Otherwise, we are in danger of making the cross of no effect. At the end of the most important council in church history, and the only one established in canon Scripture, the members concluded: **"For it seemed good to the Holy Spirit and to us to lay upon you no greater burden than these essentials: that you abstain from things sacrificed to idols and from blood and from things strangled and from fornication; if you keep yourselves free from such things, you will do well"** (Acts 15:28-29).

Were the early church leaders giving license for almost any action not included here? They did not even address such issues as stealing, jealousy, cursing, etc. Of course this does not justify those transgressions! The reason the New Testament is not meant to be just another Law is because we were to be given the liberty to *obey* the Spirit. We are not called to walk by the Law. We are called to walk in obedience to the Lord, and He will never lead us to do the things that violate His nature.

We were once married to the Law (which Paul describes in Romans 7:1-4 as our former husband), but now we have been betrothed to Christ. Can a woman who has been remarried please her present husband if she is still consumed with trying to please her former husband? Neither can we please Christ if we are continually concerned about the reaction of our "former husband," the law.

The guidelines specifically addressed in the New Testament are meant to be just enough to keep us out of trouble, while enabling us to be dependent on the Holy Spirit for guidance. The Bible was meant to facilitate our closeness to the Lord, directing us to know His voice and be dependent upon Him. But doesn't this leave a lot of room for some to abuse their liberty? Yes, and it is meant to. We do not have the freedom to obey from the heart unless we also have the freedom to disobey.

The Spirit was sent to lead us to Jesus in the Scriptures and in everything else. Reading the Scriptures without the Spirit brings only the knowledge of good and evil. Such knowledge continues to result in death today just as it did in the Garden. Man can, to a certain degree, change his outward behavior, but only God can change the heart. When we judge by the knowledge of good and evil, we will inevitably judge by externals or the form. The Lord looks upon the hearts of men, and He is looking for the heart of His Son. Those who walk by the Spirit are not too concerned with form; they seek to know by the Spirit.

We can give our all to complying with the Letter, but what good is it if we still have a foul spirit? We would be better off to be ignorant of what is "scriptural" but have a right spirit. Those who seek to comply with the biblical standards in everything do not necessarily have a wrong spirit, but they will if they are complying legalistically to biblical standards rather than seeking to be like Jesus.

Those who love Jesus, Who is the Word, will also love the Bible because it, too, is the Word. Unless the Bible is properly esteemed, we will eventually drift from God's path and have little recourse when the enemy of our soul comes with his temptations. But it must never take the place of our personal relationship to the Word Himself. The Bible must lead us to Him, not replace Him.

Used rightly, Scripture serves its purpose of communicating directly from Him to our innermost being. The Word is living water; it is a continually new wine. When it ceases to be new and fresh to us, we should first check our relationship to Him, not the translation or method we're using. When we are drawing close to Him, the Bible is not just a rule book or a history book—it is God's own love story written about us.

We Must Eat the Whole Thing

When Israel was first commanded to celebrate the Passover Feast that would set them free from Egypt, they were commanded to eat the entire lamb (see Exodus 12:8-9). If we are going to partake of Christ, we must likewise take *all* of Him. As stated, a fundamental principle of biblical interpretation is stated in Psalm 119:160, **"The *sum* of Thy word is truth."** No single biblical truth can stand alone and be isolated from the rest of the Scriptures. Each piece must fit together with the rest of the testimony of Scripture.

It was for this reason that Paul exhorts us to **"behold then the kindness *and* severity of God" (Romans 11:22).** Historically, men have gravitated to one extreme or the other in beholding *either* His kindness or His severity. We will not properly understand the nature of God unless we can see both together. Those who can only see His kindness often promote a false grace. This sometimes leads to the Lord having to use His severity with them because of their unsanctified mercy (giving mercy to the things that God disapproves of).

Those who only see His severity usually bring forth a form of godliness which cleans up the outside but is rigid and powerless to change people's hearts. God is love, but His love is often very different from human, sentimental love. God's love cannot be fully understood except in the light of His severity. Likewise, His severity cannot be fully understood apart from His kindness.

In Amos 3:7 the Lord says, **"Surely the Lord GOD does nothing unless He reveals His secret counsel to His servants the prophets."** The reference to *"prophets"* in this text is plural. We should not expect the whole truth to come from any single individual, organization or movement. Those who limit themselves to one person or organization's dogma are therefore limiting themselves to a fraction of the truth.

The Lord Jesus prayed that we would be **"perfected in unity" (John 17:23).** Until the whole church comes together in unity, we will not have the whole truth. Those who listen to only one "prophet" or leader are in danger. They are either members of a sect, a cult, or a group that is in danger of becoming one. The same is true of those who overemphasize just one truth or doctrine to the exclusion of the balancing Scriptures.

The use of individual Scriptures to build doctrines, without relating them to the rest of the biblical testimony, continues to be a primary source of false and destructive teaching in the church. There are paradoxes in Scripture, things which seem to be contradictions. These paradoxes are there by God's design and act as balances against extreme positions. The truth is usually found in the balancing tension between these paradoxes.

Paul Cain once stated that most heresies have been the result of men trying to carry to a logical conclusion what God has only revealed in part. This has certainly proven true in many cases of heresy. The Lord has revealed some things only in part for a good reason. Presently, we only need the part He has revealed in order to accomplish His purposes and walk in His salvation. The spiritual enigmas keep us dependent upon Him and His grace. This dependence is essential if we are to walk in true spiritual authority. It was

Adam and Eve's determination to understand what God had purposely kept hidden from them that resulted in the original fall. This same temptation has resulted in the fall of many more since then.

Solomon stated that **"It is the glory of God to conceal a matter, but the glory of kings is to search out a matter"** (Proverbs 25:2). The Lord desires searching, inquiring hearts with a passion to know God's ways. But those who come to know God's ways must have the utmost respect for the integrity of His Word. We must reject the tendency to add anything beyond what the Lord Himself has revealed.

It is right to love knowledge and to search for it, but we must always see knowledge as a means to an end, not the goal itself. Knowing the Lord Himself must be our goal. The goal cannot be just knowing facts about God, regardless of how true and timely those facts are. Seeking the facts without seeking a more intimate relationship with Him leads to a knowledge that **"puffs up,"** or makes proud (I Corinthians 8:1 KJV) and **"God is opposed to the proud"** (James 4:6).

Those who are coming to the true knowledge of the Lord will be increasingly humbled. The more we discover about the Lord and His ways, the bigger He gets and the smaller we become in our own eyes. Job was such a righteous man that his integrity has probably brought conviction to every man who has ever read his story. Job's discourse with his three judges reveals an understanding of the universe that science has only recently discovered. Yet when the Lord appeared to Job, he was undone.

He immediately sensed his own presumption and lack of knowledge, declaring:

> **'Who is this that hides counsel without knowledge?'**
> **"Therefore I have declared that which I did not**
> **understand,**
> **Things too wonderful for me, which I did not know."**
>
> **"I have [only] heard of Thee by the hearing of the ear;**
> **But now my eye sees Thee;**
> **Therefore I retract,**
> **And I repent in dust and ashes" (Job 42:3-6).**

When we stand before the Lord on that awesome day, how many of us are going to feel as presumptuous and undone as Job felt? How many confident assertions are going to wither and burn under the fire from His eyes? Possibly our only hope is to stop looking for the Lord and start looking *at* Him. It is right to search the Scriptures *for* the Lord, but it is just as essential that we search the Scriptures *with* Him. It is right that we preach about the Lord, but we will only be safe as we preach in the sure understanding that we are preaching in His presence.

I once heard the story of a concert pianist who was receiving a standing ovation for his performance. Awed by the spectacle of such admiration from the audience, an accompanying musician remarked to the pianist that it must be very rewarding to see such a response. "Yes, it is," declared the pianist. "But do you see that man up in the corner of the balcony? He is the master. Just a small nod from him means far more to me than this great ovation!" The pianist was playing more for the master than he was for the audience. We must do the same if we are to stay on the path of truth that leads to life.

A Moravian missionary once stated, "There are certain basic Christian truths that are essential and about which there must be agreement. On other doctrines there should be liberty, and in all things there must be charity." It should be our resolution to take an uncompromising stand on the essential doctrines of the faith and extend "the right hand of fellowship" to all who hold to them.

It should also be our resolution to protect the liberty of Christians to hold different perspectives on the nonessential doctrines. Unless we acknowledge this liberty and keep it, it will be difficult for any of us to come to a full knowledge of the truth in our hearts.

"In all things there must be charity." Nothing is impossible for our God. It would have been a small thing for Him Who stretched out the heavens to have designed everyone to believe the same thing about every doctrine. He has not done this, because it is more important for us to love one another than to believe everything exactly alike. **"The goal of our instruction is love from a pure heart and a good conscience and a sincere faith" (I Timothy 1:5).**

Chapter 26

Where Do
We Go
From Here?

There is much more to the Christian life than having our sins forgiven or even than deliverance from our sinful nature (typified by coming out of Egypt). Those are just the first steps in a long, but glorious journey. The wilderness is the place of preparation for us to enter into our calling and destiny (our Promised Land). Understanding that we are on a spiritual journey and have a destiny to fulfill is crucial if we are to accomplish the purpose for which we have been called.

To repeat Paul's word's again: **"Now these things happened to them** *as an example, and they were written for our instruction,* **upon whom the ends of the ages have come"** **(I Corinthians 10:11).** We only covered a few of the many spiritual lessons that are to be gleaned from the Old Testament. There are many more spiritual lessons to be searched out and understood. Some of these we will cover in the succeeding volumes of this series.

It is important that we understand the Old Testament because it is actually the foundation for the New Testament age of faith and grace. It is often overlooked that the Old Testament was the only Bible that the first-century church had. All of the references in the New Testament to "the Scriptures" were referring to what we call the Old Testament. It was the Old Testament that the early church used as the basis of their doctrines and their understanding of Christ.

This is not at all to belittle the importance of the New Testament, but it is basically composed of instructions and corrections to young Christians and a very brief commentary of the Old Testament. All of the doctrines of the New Testament are established by references to the Old Testament. It is the Old Testament that clearly identifies the Lord Jesus as the promised Messiah and establishes Him in His rightful place in God's plan for mankind. The apostles used the Law and the Prophets to prove their revelation of the kingdom of God, and to prove that Jesus was the promised Messiah, as we see in the following texts:

> **Now to Him who is able to establish you according to my gospel and the preaching of Jesus Christ, according to the revelation of the mystery which has been kept secret for long ages past,**

but now is manifested, and *by the Scriptures of the prophets*, according to the commandment of the eternal God, has been made known to all the nations, leading to obedience of faith (Romans 16:25-26).

And when they had set a day for him, they came to him at his lodging in large numbers; and he was explaining to them by solemnly testifying about the kingdom of God, and trying to persuade them concerning Jesus, *from both the Law of Moses and from the Prophets*, from morning until evening (Acts 28:23).

The terminology used in the New Testament to describe the place and ministry of the Lord Jesus is from the terminology used in the Law and the prophets. He is called the high priest after the Old Testament type, who was the mediator between the nation of Israel and the Lord. He is called "the Lamb of God" after the type given in the Law, the sacrificial lamb that according to the Law was to atone for the sins of the people.

When we think of the Law, we usually think of all the burdensome commandments, but they were actually just a small part of the purpose for the Law. The main purpose of the Law was to be a **"schoolmaster to bring us to Christ"** (Galatians 4:24 KJV). The Law actually contains a prophetic blueprint for the New Testament church. The first-century church could easily understand all the terms like "high priest" and "Lamb of God" because they had the types right in their midst. We still have The Old Testament as a part of our Bible so that we can search out the meanings of such types. It is just as important that we understand them today as it was for the first-century church.

When the Lord chastised the two men on the road to Emmaus, He said, **"Oh foolish men and slow of heart to believe in** *all that the prophets have spoken...and beginning with Moses and with all the prophets, He explained to them the things concerning Himself in ALL the Scriptures"* **(Luke 24:25, 27).** Earlier He had said, **"For if you believed Moses, you would believe Me, for He wrote of Me.** *But if you do not believe his writings, how will you believe My words?"* **(John 5:46-47)**

Through the Law given to Moses, and the prophets who expounded upon that Law, we are provided with a very clear picture of God's plan for us. The place of the Lord Jesus is clearly typified, and we are told how we are to relate to Him. Everything that Jesus did and every major doctrine established in the New Testament had a foundation in the Old Testament.

When we speak of the Old Testament being the foundation for the New Testament, we are obviously not implying that the keeping of the Law is the foundation for Christianity. Jesus said, **"For all the prophets and** *the Law prophesied* **until John"** **(Matthew 11:13).** The Law was a *prophecy!* The Law was a prophetic outline of the entire church age, given with breathtaking accuracy thousands of years before the time of its fulfillment.

That is what was meant by the Lord's statement that **"not the smallest letter or stroke shall pass away from the Law, *until all is accomplished"* (Matthew 5:18).** Even the smallest details of the Law were prophesies that have been meticulously coming to pass for the past two thousand years, and most of the church has been completely ignorant of this! Most of the church has not understood what has been happening through the unfolding of history because she did not understand this one simple truth—that the Law was a prophecy.

We can historically see how different aspects of the Law have already passed away because they have been fulfilled. When Jesus fulfilled the sacrificial mandates of the Law with His sacrifice on Calvary, soon thereafter the ceremonial sacrifices ceased to be offered. Likewise, after the church was instituted—the temple **"made without hands" (Mark 14:58)**—the physical temple in Jerusalem was destroyed.

Because the church has generally failed to understand the prophetic nature of the Law, we have not been able to really understand the prophetic books of the Bible, especially those filled with symbolism like the books of Daniel and Revelation. As Daniel was told concerning his own prophecy, **"But as for you, Daniel, conceal these words and seal up the book *until the end of time"* (Daniel 12:4).**

One of the surest signs that we have in fact come to the end of time is that these books are now being opened to our understanding. The key to understanding these books, without falling into free association and confusion, is to understand how the Law was a prophecy. All of the prophetic symbolism in the prophetic books is established in the types and shadows of the Law.

When we start to see history prophesied so clearly in the Law, it brings into sharp focus the plan of God for the last-day ministry of the church. This imparts the faith and confidence that we are going to need in order to accomplish our destiny. Jesus saw Himself in all the Scriptures, from Moses through all of the prophets. When He said **"It is written,"** it came with authority, because He knew who He was and He knew His plan and destiny by what was written. As we begin to clearly see how the Lord also outlined *our* destiny in the Scriptures, we too will begin to move in greater faith, boldness and authority. The deeper our foundations, the more that can be built upon them.

Many today are running about seeking a word from God, when the greatest Word that He will ever speak to them is gathering dust on the shelf. The angels who can observe us must consider this one of the greatest of human tragedies.

The last few chapters were an attempt to dispel some of the major roadblocks that have been erected to keep the common people from seeking the priceless treasures in the Scriptures. What makes something valuable is that it is either rare, or hard to get. Knowledge can be cheap, but the priceless treasures of the knowledge of God's ways come from careful and diligent searching.

Every great spiritual awakening, revival or reformation in history has come because the people were awakened to the truth of the Scriptures. However, the greatest move of God of all time is still in the future, not the past. Like all the others, this move of God will be ignited by an opening of the Scriptures, and a love for the Scriptures will perpetuate it.

Every believer can probably remember that in their times of greatest spiritual advancement there was a corresponding hunger for the Word of God. The underlying passion that drives us in such advancement is the desire to be closer to Jesus, who is the Word of God. Because Jesus is the Word of God, the more we love Him, the more we will love the Word of God.

When the church is encouraged, she spreads spiritual seeds all over the land. Nothing encourages the church as much as the presence of the Lord. All that it takes for us to have His presence is for us to seek Him. If we draw near to Him, He promises to draw near to us (James 4:8). The key to true and lasting revival is a church that has maintained her first love.

When a person falls in love, all they want to do is talk about the one they love. Anyone who has had the experience of having that passionate love knows that there is nothing else quite like it that can be experienced in this life. This is called "first love," or the way love is at first. Very few learn the secret of keeping that passion going, but those who do have the most fulfilling marriages and lives.

Every Christian experiences this "first love" with Jesus immediately after conversion. Some keep this feeling longer than others, but like human marriages, most lose their initial passion in time. Most who lose it do so because they are distracted from Jesus by all the spiritual activities they are taught are a necessary part of "the Christian life." Soon they start worshiping the temple of the Lord (the church) instead of the Lord of the temple.

The danger is that we can easily become like the bride who became more devoted to her home than to the husband for whom she was keeping the home. If this bride would return to her first love with her husband, she would keep the home even better than she would by making the home her first priority. Love does change and mature, but we can measure the quality of our marriage by how much of our "first love" passion we have maintained.

The grace of God is about to restore this first love to His church. He is about to release the most contagious thing that there has ever been on the earth—the love that He has for His Son. There is nothing in this world that is more contagious than someone who is getting closer to the Lord. There is nothing in creation more infectious than the love of God. Everyone who comes in contact with those so infected will likewise catch it! For those who catch this passion there is no cure, and they cannot stand to live without getting closer to the Lord.

The Lord will not return until the bride says, **"Come"** **(Revelation 22:17).** Most of the church does not really want the Lord to come back yet—it would upset too many of their plans! But we are about to fall so in love with Him again that we will become consumed in our longing to see Him face to face. When we are not worshiping Him, we will be praying to Him. When we are not praying to Him, we will be pouring over the Scriptures just to read about Him. Witnessing will then be real and spontaneous, because we simply will not be able to stop talking about Him.

The veil of religious pressure, hype and spiritual politics are going to be swept away by this love for the Son of God. The last-day leadership of the church will be composed of those who are the closest to the Lord and who are devoted to helping others get close to Him. That is, in its most simple terms, the qualification for true spiritual leadership.

This does not negate biblical scholarship, but it will establish it as genuine scholarship that is a love for the Truth Himself. When this love compels us to search more zealously and more deeply, so that we might know Him better and serve Him more perfectly, we will find the well of Living Water that never runs dry.

We are on a journey, but we must not continue to go in aimless circles in the wilderness. We must go through the wilderness to get to the Promised Land, but we do not want to stay in the wilderness any longer than we have to! We must relentlessly keep our vision and our course directed toward our destiny. In the fourth book in this series, we will continue the journey. But first, in Volume III we will take time to study the most important reason for the wilderness experience—building a habitation for the Lord.

It was in the wilderness that Israel constructed the tabernacle so that the Lord could dwell among His people. Some of the most powerful and important prophetic truths found in Scripture are highlighted in the instructions the Lord gave for the place that He would inhabit. Getting to the Promised Land is important, but first we must take the time to properly build His habitation so that He might dwell among us. Dwelling in the presence of the Lord is more important than possessing our promises, for even the most glorious Promised Land would be a terrible place without Him.

BIBLIOGRAPHY

Baker, *Protestant Biblical Interpretation*
Bartleman, *Another Wave of Revival*
Bhayr, *Getting the Word Out*
Billheimer, *Destined for the Cross*
Billheimer, *Destined for the Throne*
Bonhoeffer, *Creation and Fall*
Bonhoeffer, *Life Together*
Bonhoeffer, *The Cost of Discipleship*
Bonhoeffer, *The Way to Freedom*
Booker, *Blow a Trumpet In Zion*
Booker, *Radical Christian Living*
Bridges, *The Practice of Godliness*
Bridges, *The Pursuit of Holiness*

Brown, *How Saved Are We?*

Brown, *The End of American Gospel Enterprise*

Card, *Immanuel*

Chantry, *Today's Gospel*

Christenson, *A Message to the Charismatic Movement*

Colson, *Against the Night*

Colson, *Kingdoms in Conflict*

Colson, *Loving God*

Conn, *Inerrancy and Hermeneutics*

Conner/Malmin, *Interpreting the Scriptures*

Davidson/Rees-Mogg, *The Great Reckoning*

Dawson, *Taking Our Cities for God*

Doron, *The Mystery of Israel and the Church*

Drummond, *The Changed Life*

Drummond, *The Greatest Thing in the World*

Edwards, *The Divine Romance*

Edwards, *The Life of David Brainerd*

FAA, *The Airman's Information Manual*

Finney, *Finney on Revival*

Finney, *Love Is Not a Special Way of Feeling*

Flanagan, *Before the Battle*

Frangipane, *Holiness, Truth and the Presence of God*

Frangipane, *The Three Battlegrounds*

Frankl, *Man's Search for Reason*

Fromke, *Unto Full Stature*

Grant, *The Blood of the Moon*

Hall, *The Church In Transition*

Havner, *The Best of Vance Havner*

Hawking, *A Brief History of Time*

Hayford, *A Passion for Fulness*

Henley, *Form or Frenzy*
Hession, *From Shadow to Substance*
Hian, *The Making of a Leader*
Inrig, *Hearts of Iron, Feet of Clay*
Jacobsen, *A Passion for God's Presence*
Juster and Intrater, *Israel, the Church and the Last Days*
Katz, *Reality*
Kaung, *The Splendor of His Ways*
Kendall, *God Meant It For Good*
Kenney, *His Rule in His Church*
Kinne, *Intervention In the Ecclesia*
Kruup, *The Church Triumphant*
Ladd, *The Blessed Hope*
Ladd, *The Gospel of the Kingdom*
Lange, *The Covenant of the Kingdom*
Lange, *The Gospel of the Kingdom*
Lange, *The Sabbath*
Lawrence, *The Practice of the Presence of God*
Leenhouts, *Competition of the Altars*
Lewis, *Mere Christianity*
Lewis, *Miracles*
Lewis, *Reflections on the Psalms*
Lewis, *The Weight of Glory*
Lord, *Eagles and Turkeys*
Lord, *Hearing God*
Lord, *Soul Care*
Loosley, *When the Church Was Young*
Lucado, *The Applause of Heaven*
Martin, *John Knox*
McClung, *Discovering Your Destiny*

McClung, *Effective Evangelism*
McClung, *Holiness and the Spirit of the Age*
McClung, *The Father Heart of God*
McGaw, *Praying Hyde*
McKeever, *Be Prepared*
Morris, *A Biblical Manual on Science and Creation*
Mosley, *Manifest Victory*
Mosley, *Perfect Everything*
Mosley, *The Three Virtues*
Muggeridge, *Jesus Rediscovered*
Mumford, *Handling God's Glory*
Murray, *Humility*
Murray, *The Inner Life*
Murray, *Abide in Christ*
Murray, *Be Perfect*
Murray, *Let Us Draw Near*
Murray, *Like Christ*
Murray, *With Christ in the School Of Prayer*
Naisbitt and Aburdene, *Megatrends 2000*
Nee, *Changed Into His Likeness*
Nee, *Sit, Walk, Stand*
Nee, *Ye Search the Scriptures*
Neighbour, *Where Do We Go From Here*
Nori, *How to Find God's Love*
Ortiz, *Cry of the Human Heart*
Ortiz, *Living With Jesus Today*
Passantino, *Witch Hunt*
Pittman, *Placebo*
Porter, *Luther—Selected Political Writings*
Ravenhill, D. *For God's Sake—Grow Up*

Ravenhill, L. *America Is Too Young to Die*

Ravenhill, L. *Meat for Men*

Ravenhill, L. *Tried and Transfigured*

Ravenhill, L. *Why Revival Tarries*

Renner, *Merchandising the Anointing*

Robinson, *Biblical Preaching*

Robison, *Winning the Real War*

Room, *Wanted: Your Daily Life*

Rumble, *Crucible of the Future*

Sawyer, *All About the Moravians*

Sawyer, *These Fifteen—Pioneers of the Moravian Church*

Schaeffer, *Escape From Reason*

Schaeffer, *Genesis In Space and Time*

Schaeffer, *No Little People*

Schaeffer, *The Church at the End of the Twentieth Century*

Searle, *David Brainerd's Personal Testimony*

Shorrosh, *Islam Revealed*

Solzhenitsyn, *A World Split Apart*

Sparks, *The School of Christ*

Sparks, *Words of Wisdom and Revelation*

Spurgeon, *All of Grace*

Sumrall, *New Wine Bottles*

Synan, *In the Latter Days*

Synan, *The Twentieth Century Pentecostal Explosion*

Taylor, *The Secret of the Stairs*

Toffler, *Power Shift*

Tolstoy, *Anna Karanina*

Tolstoy, *The Kingdom of God Is Within You*

Tolstoy, *War and Peace*

Tosini, *Is There Not a Cause*

Tournier, *Reflections*
Tozer, *Knowledge of the Holy*
Verdun, *The Reformers and Their Stepchildren*
Virgo, *Restoration in the Church*
Wagner, *Strategies for Church Growth*
Wallis, *A Biblical Agenda*
Wallis, *Revival*
Wallis, *The Radical Christian*
Warnock, *Beauty for Ashes*
Weinlick, *Count Zinzendorf*

The Morning Star
PROPHETIC BULLETIN

In order to swiftly promulgate important, prophetic messages to the body of Christ, we have instituted this service. The primary contributors will be **Paul Cain, Bobby Conner, Bob Jones** and **Rick Joyner.** Other proven prophetic ministries will contribute at times. *Distribution will be at irregular times dictated by the timeliness and importance of the messages received.*

Only...$5.00!
for a 1 year subscription
Catalog No. MSPB-001
$7.00 USD for foreign subscriptions.

CALL 1-800-542-0278
——— TO ORDER ———
CREDIT CARD ORDERS ONLY.